THE SPIRITUAL JOURNEY AND THE DEEPER LIFE

JAMES P. DANAHER

Apocryphile Press
PO Box 255
Hannacroix, NY 12087
www.apocryphilepress.com

Copyright © 2025 by James Danaher
Printed in the United States of America
ISBN 978-1-965646-33-5 | paper
ISBN 978-1-965646-34-2 | ePub

No part of this book may be reproduced, stored in a retrieval system, or transmitted in any form or by any means—electronic, mechanical, photocopy, recording, or otherwise—without written permission of the author and publisher, except for brief quotations in printed reviews.

The author would like to thank Janeen Jones for her excellent editing.

Please join our mailing list at www.apocryphilepress.com/free. We'll keep you up-to-date on all our new releases, and we'll also send you a FREE BOOK. Visit us today!

CONTENTS

Preface   v

1. The Historical Origins of Christianity and the Deeper Life   1
2. The Two Levels of Consciousness and the Deeper Life   12
3. The Spiritual Journey and the Death of the False Self   21
4. The Two Loves and the Deeper Life   38
5. Our Beliefs and Righteousness versus the Deeper Life   50
6. Our Transformation into the Deeper life to which Jesus Calls Us   67
7. The Practice of the Deeper Life and the Words of Jesus   85
8. Synopsis of the Spiritual Journey and the Deeper Life   104

Epilogue   119

PREFACE
THE TWO TRUTHS

Our concept of truth comes in two distinct forms: epistemological and ontological. Those are two big words for the fact that human beings have always been interested in truth as both something to know and something to be.

Aristotle (384–322 BC) was the great advocate for truth as something to know. He claimed that human beings were involved in the three major activities of making, doing, and knowing. When we make, we want to make what is beautiful, when we do, we want to do what is good, and when we know, we want to know what is true. The epistemological truth of what we should know and believe about Christianity has been argued over since the early days of Christianity and today there are over forty thousand Christian denominations or sects worldwide, each claiming to *know* the ultimate truth of Christianity.

There is, however, another notion concerning the ultimate truth of Christianity which is not an epistemological truth—something to know and believe—but an ontologically true way to *be*. God may ultimately be a great mystery that is beyond our knowing, but many have argued that the ultimate truth of

Christianity is not about our knowing God, but about our being like God in the terms that Jesus describes.

The truth of our being is not something to know but a way of being that reflects our loves. Before Aristotle's notion of truth as something to know became popular, both Socrates and Plato believed that truth was not merely something to know, but rather a way to be. Ontological truth, or truth as a way of being, was also the notion of truth that was the focus of several teachers from the East who arose around the same time as Socrates and Plato. Lao Tzu, Confucius, and Buddha all lived at approximately the same time, roughly five centuries before the time of Jesus. What all these men had in common was that they didn't think of truth as something to know, but as something to be. Jesus was in that tradition rather than the Aristotelian tradition of truth as something to know. Sadly, many of the churches that bear Jesus' name operate out of that Aristotelian tradition of truth, resting their faith in what they claim to know and believe is the truth of the gospel, whether it be the Nicene Creed, the Salvation Gospel, or the beliefs of Southern Baptists, Roman Catholics, or Jehovah Witnesses.

Of course, Jesus' words are never about what we should know in terms of truth, but *how* we should be in order to resemble our Father, God. The search for truth as an ultimate way to be requires change or transformation, since our original way of being was acquired through a process of acculturation, whereby we largely learned a way of being that was appropriate to the unique historical and cultural settings of our lives. Some may buck against this cultural way of being, but the serious search for a deeper or truer way to be doesn't usually begin until later in life. The reason that search usually doesn't begin until much later in life, if it begins at all, is because the deeper life to which Jesus calls us requires an enormous transformation from the way we were socialized during childhood, adolescence, and early adulthood. Such a transformation can be painful; many try to avoid it by believing that we only need to change what we believe *in*—that is, that the truth is something to know and believe. Faith as a true belief, rather than a way of being that is contrary to the way of the world, is enormously popular, since it requires little more than a new idea which we hold to be true and sacred.

Popular religion tells us that we can avoid the painful transformation into a deeper life with a truth that is simply something to know and believe. The Nicene Creed (325 CE), and later versions of that creed were the initial version of popular Christianity, which required nothing more than a right belief rather than a transformed being. There have been many versions of popular Christianity over the last two thousand years. Today, the most popular version of contemporary Christianity is the Salvation Gospel, which claims that salvation is not a transformation into a deeper life, but simply a belief in the factual truth that Jesus died as payment for our sins: that it is *that* belief that removes our sin and makes us ready for heaven just as we are. Accepting a new belief as factually true is very different from accepting a new way of being, since a new way of being requires an end to our habitual way of being. It is much more than just a new idea that we identify with as true. The Salvation Gospel is enormously popular since it requires nothing but a new epistemological belief. But the deeper life to which Jesus calls his followers ultimately requires a radically different way of being than the way the world has taught. Truth as something to know and believe requires minimal change to our being and adds value to our identity because it allows us to see ourselves as more than other people because we feel assured of God's forgiveness because of our belief.

The truth of our being, on the other hand, is a living, dynamic truth that is never simply something to know and believe. Jesus is always inviting us into a deeper level of being in God and God being in us, rather than our being in the world and the world being in us. How far we want to go into this deeper life to which Jesus calls us is ultimately what faith is all about. Eternal life is not on a pass/fail basis determined by what we believe to be factually true about God, salvation, and eternal life. The deeper life to which Jesus calls his followers is ultimately about how much of Jesus' living words have come to life within us.

Our spiritual journey into the deeper life to which Jesus calls us may begin as a simple belief in the objective truth of the gospel—whatever that means at the time—but the words of Jesus are always calling us to a deeper life. The call to that deeper life is hard to hear for people who love the worldly life they have created for themselves, since it is easy to see themselves as the god or creator of that life. In the time of Jesus, both the Pharisees and Romans had trouble making sense of Jesus' words, since he addressed who they were in God rather than who they were in the world. In fact, the beauty of Jesus' words can only be seen from the perspective of who we are in God rather than who we are in the world, since, from the perspective we inherited from the world, it makes no sense to forgive everyone,[1] judge no one,[2] and love even our enemies.[3]

There is, however, a level of consciousness from which we can see the beauty of Jesus' words, but that level of consciousness must be practiced if it is to become the dominant level of consciousness out of which we live our lives. The way we come into an awareness of this deeper level of being is through the practice of being alone with God and turning off the constant flow of thoughts which occupy the mind that connects us to the world. This is prayer at its deepest level, but it must be practiced continually if it is to become the dominant level of consciousness out of which we live our lives.

Our journey into this deeper life to which Jesus calls his followers ultimately leads to the death of the ego or false self. This self is something we ourselves created in order to be successful in the world, to be in a better state than our neighbors—and especially a better state than our enemies. It is shaped by our cultural ideas of survival of the fittest, athletic competition with its winning and losing, grades in school, and a competitive economy; all of these contribute to the socialization that encourages us to be better than our neighbors and our enemies.

Throughout our childhood, adolescence, and early adulthood our egos are at work trying to make a place for ourselves in this competitive world. We want a place that is better than our neighbors' and our enemies'. Of course, this activity of the ego is often not operating on a conscious level. But unconsciously, it underlies so much of what we do and who we become. If we are successful at creating a self that appears to be more than others in terms of wealth, power, prestige, talent, beauty, or righteous beliefs, we tend to love that false self because we are its god and creator. But the living words of Jesus can never take root within that life—only within the deeper life of who we are in God and who God is in us. Jesus' words cannot take root within the self that we have created to be in the world, but only in that deeper life of who we are in God and who God is in us. This is the deeper life that is the end of the spiritual journey. We all get to choose how far we wish to go into this deeper life. What greatly determines how far we go into this deeper life to which Jesus calls us is largely determined by how much we disidentify with the life that we have created to be in the world: to be better off than others.

The ego creates a life in the world where we make ourselves appear to be better than our neighbors and our enemies. Religious faith is a belief that supposedly makes us better than other human beings in God's sight. It's very appealing to the ego, but that self that we create can never give root to Jesus' living words, which require a deeper life than the life we have created to succeed in the world.

Jesus' words to his followers are living words meant to come to life within us, but the living words of Jesus cannot come to life within the person we have created to be in the world, because that person is intent upon being more than both its neighbors and its enemies, while Jesus' words can only take root within someone who is less than their neighbors and enemies.

The spiritual journey to which Jesus calls us is all about becoming less rather than more.

We might like to believe that our sacred true beliefs make us better than other human beings, but the living words of Jesus to his disciples can never take root in that life, and for that reason Jesus is always calling us to that deeper life, when we were in God and God was in us, before the world began making us into its likeness. Becoming less is essentially a matter of becoming an empty vessel through whom God's love, mercy, and forgiveness might pass to the world without interference from our judgments; it is an empty vessel that has no love of the things of the world that give us the appearance of being better than our neighbors and our enemies. This is the ultimate end and purpose of the Gospel. Jesus came into the world to bring his kingdom to earth, and for two thousand years there have been individuals willing to be those empty vessels fit for use by God to that ultimate purpose.

The spiritual journey to which Jesus calls his followers may begin by believing that Jesus has suffered and died as payment for your sins. This supposes that the purpose of the gospel is to allow our eternal existence to be the one that we ourselves created for life in the world—except with our sins forgiven. Jesus, however, is always calling us to something much more than that, since an eternal existence centered around the false self that we have created would be a hellish eternity.

The deeper life to which Jesus calls us is not simply a matter of acquiring forgiveness as a reward for our belief that

Jesus' payment for our sins is a fact. Rather, it is a matter of transforming into beings capable of being Jesus' mercy, forgiveness, and love to the world. Only empty vessels, devoid of ego, can have God's mercy, forgiveness, and love pass through them to the world, just as they themselves received such love from Jesus.

We are not transformed by our beliefs or knowledge of the truth, but by Jesus' words revealing the depth of our sin, and our repentance over those deeper sins, followed by our own experience of God's mercy and forgiveness always being deeper still. Jesus doesn't tell us how to get our sins forgiven, but how to experience mercy and forgiveness on ever deeper levels so we might be transformed into his merciful and forgiving likeness. This deeper life to which Jesus calls his followers ultimately requires the death of the ego, the self-created false self, that which the world has taught us to create. The "righteousness" of being more than our neighbors and enemies is often experienced in the early stages of the spiritual journey, but the spiritual journey always leads toward the death of that false self that we have created to be in the world, so that our deeper life in God might come forth.

This quest for righteousness, the beginning of the spiritual journey, can last for years. In time, however, if we spend enough time alone with God and Jesus' words, we begin to see how different the self-created, world-inspired false self is from the deeper life to which Jesus calls us. Getting back to who we were in God and who God was in us before the world began making us into its likeness is what the spiritual journey is all about. This has been what Christian mystics and saints have been about for the last two thousand years. Of course, we do not begin the spiritual journey as mystics or saints. Our first encounters with God are almost always from the perspective of the false self, and those God experiences will tend to inflate the ego, making it impossible to love others in the same way we love ourselves. Jesus teaches us to give ourselves away to others in the same way that Jesus gave himself away to others. That goes against everything the world has taught us about loving ourselves and competing over the scarce resources that the world tells us will make us of more substance than our neighbors and our enemies.

Jesus, however, tells us of a deeper life that takes us in a different direction from what the world had set us on. Early in the spiritual journey we are largely unaware of a deeper life, which only comes about through spending time in the silence of God's presence and Jesus' words. The reason Jesus' words are so important is because they alone tell us that there is something wrong with the understanding that the world has given us, and that understanding is what keeps us from the deeper life to which Jesus calls us.

Jesus tells us that God is our Father and desires his children to be as he is in terms of love, forgiveness, and mercy. Of course, from the perspective the world has given us, it is hard to see a benefit in loving our enemies,[4] forgiving everyone,[5] and judging no one.[6] We need to develop a deeper perspective than the one the world has given us, and that is exactly what Jesus gives. To see the beauty of Jesus' words, we need to practice the deeper life of being in Jesus and Jesus being in us.

This is the deeper life to which Jesus calls us, but it must be practiced if it is to become the dominant level of consciousness out of which we live our lives. This deeper life is not simply a matter of being forgiven, but about being transformed into the instruments of Jesus' mercy, forgiveness, and love to the world. Only empty vessels are capable of God's mercy, forgiveness, and love passing through them without interference from the judgments of the false self.

We are not transformed by our beliefs or knowledge of the truth, but by the words of Jesus revealing the depth of our sin, and our repentance over those deepest sins, followed by the experience of God's mercy and forgiveness always being deeper still. Jesus doesn't tell us how to get our sins forgiven, but how to experience mercy and forgiveness on ever deeper levels so we might be transformed into his merciful and forgiving likeness.

This deeper life to which Jesus calls his followers ultimately requires the death of the ego and the false self that it creates to be in the world, and to be in the world in a better state than others. This righteousness of being more than our neighbors and our enemies is often experienced in the early stages of the spiritual journey, but the spiritual journey always leads toward the death of that false self that we have created to be in the world in a better state than our neighbors and our enemies. This is the quest for righteousness from which we usually begin the spiritual journey. In time, however, if we spend enough time alone with God and Jesus' words, we begin to gain access to the deeper life of who we were in God before the world began making us into its likeness, where survival of the fittest and competition over scarce resources are intended to make us better than our neighbors and especially better than our enemies.

---

1. Matthew 6:44.
2. Matthew 7:1-2.
3. Matthew 5:44.
4. Matthew 5:44.
5. Matthew 6:15.
6. Matthew 7:1-2.

CHAPTER I
THE HISTORICAL ORIGINS OF CHRISTIANITY AND THE DEEPER LIFE

Historically, Christianity began as a particular *way of being*, which Jesus had taught his disciples. In fact, this way of being was initially referred to as The Way, and these people of The Way were only first called Christians in the year 100 CE. This way of being based upon the teachings of Jesus was spread throughout the Roman world initially by his disciples and later by their disciples, who created churches throughout the Roman world. Many of these early Christians were persecuted and even martyred for their commitment to this strange way that Jesus had taught his followers to embody.

With the end of the Apostolic period around 100 CE a great variety of beliefs began to appear concerning the nature of Jesus and his relationship with God. This period, beginning in the second century of the Christian era and continuing into the fourth century, came to be known as the Ante-Nicene period, which was full of differing opinions concerning the divinity of Jesus and his relationship to God, who Jesus referred to as Father.

In time, the Roman persecution of Christians eased and

eventually the Roman Emperor Constantine (280–337) made all religions legal with the edict of Milan in 313. There are also legends about Constantine having a vision of a Christian symbol which helped him win a battle, thus bringing about his conversion to Christianity. Others have argued that Constantine did not become a Christian until his deathbed in 337. Whatever was Constantine's personal story, Constantine did call for the Counsel of Nicaea (325) which was the first attempt to set forth the basic orthodox beliefs of Christianity with the Nicene Creed. Prior to the Nicene Creed different Christian churches had different beliefs concerning the nature of Jesus and his relationship to God. In the year 380, the Roman Emperor Theodosius (347-395) issued the Edict of Thessalonica, which made Nicene Christianity the official church of the Roman state. Christian churches which refused to conform to the beliefs of Nicene Christianity were condemned by the Roman church and their property was confiscated.

Thus, with the Nicene creed, it became popular to associate Christianity with beliefs rather than the strange way that Jesus had taught his followers to be. Of course, this idea of religious faith as a set of beliefs concerning Jesus' relationship to God was much more popular than a Way of being in conformity with the strange teachings of Jesus to forgive everyone,[1] judge no one,[2] and love even one's enemies.[3] Religious faith as a set of beliefs that make some people better than other people became enormously popular and spread throughout the Roman Empire, but it had the negative effect of undermining the most basic teachings of Jesus to love your neighbor[4] (and even your enemy[5]) in the same way you love yourself.[6]

A religious belief that promises to add something to both our earthly and eternal existence has always been more popular than the radically different way Jesus called on his followers to incarnate. This difference between Christianity as a way of being and Christianity as a set of beliefs is not necessarily to argue that these are two different forms of Christianity, but rather, that these two different ways of understanding Christianity represent different stages in the spiritual journey.

The spiritual journey almost always begins from the perspective of the person we have created ourselves to be in the world. The world teaches us to love ourselves and become better than our neighbor, and especially better than our enemies. The world teaches us to compete for the scarce resources of wealth, power, prestige, talent, strength, or beauty, so we might be seen by other human beings as more than our neighbors and especially more than our enemies. Jesus, however, tells us these are all the illusions of the false self that we have created in the hope of becoming more than our neighbors and enemies, both in our own minds and in the minds of others. None of the world's values are anything like the divine, eternal qualities which Jesus' words to his disciples describe.

> If you abide in me, and my words abide in you, ask whatever you wish, and it will be done for you. My Father is glorified by this, that you bear much fruit and become my disciples. As the Father has loved me, so I have loved you; abide in my love. If you keep my commandments, you will abide in my love.[7]

We, however, keep Jesus' commandments differently than Jesus did. Jesus, by the time he was thirty years of age, had completed the spiritual journey and was no longer under the influence of an ego, but had become that perfectly empty vessel through whom God's mercy, forgiveness, and love might pass to the world. Jesus did that perfectly. We do it through continual repentance over our repeated failures because we are not yet at the end of our journeys—unless we get stuck believing that our beliefs have made us sinless and therefore righteous. Believing that righteousness is the ultimate end of the spiritual journey is the great sin of the ego and its desire to be more than the rest of

God's children. The ultimate solution to this sin is the death of the ego, but since it usually takes a lifetime for the ego to die, and the dying process doesn't even usually begin until the second half of life, the way we deal with the ego is through repentance over our being led through so much of our life by our self-concern rather than our concern to be God's instruments of mercy, forgiveness, and love to the world.

This is the deeper life to which Jesus calls his followers, but this deeper life cannot be experienced from the perspective the world has given us. Even the disciples themselves didn't initially understand this deeper life. At the end of John's Gospel, Jesus tells his disciples, "On that day you will know that I am in my Father, and you in me, and I in you."[8] Jesus speaks these words to his disciples shortly before his crucifixion, so knowing that they were in Jesus and Jesus was in them did not happen in their first three years of discipleship. The deeper life to which Jesus calls his followers is something that happens as part of a transformative journey over the course of a lifetime. We almost all initially follow Jesus from the perspective of the person that we have created to be in the world. From that perspective, faith as a set of beliefs concerning Jesus and his relationship to God is more attractive than the strange way that Jesus had taught his followers to love everyone in the same way they love themselves. From the perspective the world has given us, we can accept new beliefs concerning Jesus and God, but a radically different way to love requires a spiritual journey of transformation that usually takes a lifetime.

After having spent three years with Jesus, Jesus tells his disciples that "...the Holy Spirit, whom the Father will send in my name, will teach you everything, and remind you of all that I have said to you."[9] We do not immediately get the teachings of Jesus because the beauty of his words cannot be seen from the perspective the world has given us. That is because the teachings of Jesus are not compatible with the life that we have created for ourselves to be in the world. For most of us, our childhood, adolescence, and early adulthood have taught us how to be in the world and survive and flourish according to the world's ways. Jesus' heavenly words, however, can never take root within that person. Indeed, Jesus' words to his disciples can only take root within that deeper life of who we were in God and who God was in us before the world began making us into its likeness. This is why Jesus tells Nicodemus, "...no one can see the kingdom of God without being born from above."[10]

Just as there is a birth into this world, there is a birth into the heavenly realm as well. Some people wait until their deathbed to experience it, others are luckier to have experienced that death experience sooner. This born-again experience can happen in an instant, but coming to identify with that deeper life of who we were in God and who God was in us before the world began making us into its likeness requires a lifetime of dying to the person we have created to be in the world. Without the born-again experience being followed by a lifetime of dying to the life that the ego has created for itself in the world, the idea of being in Jesus and Jesus being in us will merely inflate the ego and give us the idea that we are more than other human beings, superior to our neighbors, and especially superior to our enemies. The ultimate purpose of the gospel, however, is to make us less than other human beings so God's love, mercy, and forgiveness might flow through us to the world without interference from the judgments of the ego concerning who is deserving and who is not deserving of God's mercy, forgiveness, and love.

Of course, popular churches must appeal to the false selves that we have created to be in the world, if they are to have any popularity, since this is the place from which almost all of us begin the spiritual journey, and the place so many of us get stuck. Thus, popular churches offer beliefs that purport to make us more righteous than other people in God's sight, which has great appeal to the egoic self. Jesus' teachings, however, reveal our sin at ever deeper levels. This is intended to convince us that we, like Paul, are chief among sinners.[11] The great benefit of seeing ourselves as chief among sinners is that with that experience comes another: that as deep as our sins may be, God's mercy and forgiveness are always deeper still. The end of the spiritual journey is not to make us righteous by having our sins forgiven because we profess the right beliefs, but to make us into the agents of Jesus' mercy, forgiveness, and love to the world. We only become such agents by seeing our own sin and our own need for mercy, forgiveness, and love at ever deeper levels. It is only our repentance over Jesus' words that begins our transformation into that deeper life to which Jesus calls his followers.

God is Love, but what limits God's love passing through us to the world is our lack of mercy and forgiveness for those that we judge unworthy of God's love. This is the arrogance and pride of the false self or ego, which we have created to be in the world. Popular forms of Christianity appeal to the false self and tell us that God wants us to be better than our neighbors and our enemies. All we need is to know what to believe in—our sins will be paid for at the mere cost of a belief. What ego wouldn't believe that? A free ticket to paradise in exchange for a professed belief.

Jesus, however, tells a very different story. Although a professed belief is not necessarily a bad start, there is way more to the gospel than a belief. The gospel is about a spiritual journey into the deeper life to which Jesus calls us. What makes the gospel so different from the earlier parts of the Bible is that Jesus is not telling us how to live a righteous life in the world, but how to bring Jesus' heavenly kingdom to earth.

In the early stages of the spiritual journey to which Jesus calls us, we still identify with the false self that we have created to be in the world, and we care little for anything apart from that self, which we have created to be in the world. From such a perspective, our prayers are requests that God would give us the desires of that life that we have created to be in the world. But there is a deeper life, and if we spend time alone with God and Jesus' words, we begin to become aware of this deeper life to which Jesus calls his followers.

God's ultimate desire is to create beings like himself in terms of mercy, forgiveness, and love. Of course, God had created angelic beings who resembled God in this regard, but they were made to be merciful, forgiving, and loving. To create beings who more closely resembled their creator, God would have to create beings who had the freedom to create their own eternal nature by the things they chose to love, just like God created his own eternal nature by the things he chose to love. Such a creation would require a world where love came in two very distinct forms: one resembling the love that Jesus revealed by giving himself away in acts of forgiveness, mercy, and love; and another where what we love is intended to make us more than our neighbors and our enemies. This second love is the love that connects us to the world rather than God, and is directed at things like wealth, power, prestige, physical beauty, strength, or righteous beliefs which make us appear in our own minds and the minds of other people to be of more value than our neighbors, and especially of more value than our enemies. This is the love of self rather than the love of others, and we are living in this world. Here love of self is reinforced by ideas like survival of the fittest, competition, and a market economy, where "it is not from the benevolence of the butcher, the brewer, or the baker, that we expect our dinner, but from their regard to their own interest. We address ourselves, not to their humanity but to their self-love..."[12]

This is the way of the world, and the way the world has taught us to be. When we are looking for a date, a spouse, a job, or a friend, we try to convince other people that we would be a better date, spouse, employee, or friend than others that they might choose. Successful people are good at convincing us that they would be a better choice than choosing other people to satisfy those desires within us. Jesus, however, calls us to a deeper life than the one unto which the world has molded us. Jesus' words describe a life of giving ourselves away to others in acts of mercy, forgiveness, and love. That cannot be done from the level of consciousness that we have acquired by being in the world, but there is a level of consciousness from which we can see how beautiful it is to forgive everyone, judge no one, and love even one's enemies. Of course, we must come to identify with that deeper level of consciousness rather than the one we have acquired by being in the world. The spiritual journey is the road back to who we were in God and who God was in us before the world began making us into its likeness rather than the likeness of our Father God.

The reason we have to make this journey back to who we were in God and who God was in us is because Jesus' words can never take root and produce heavenly fruit within the person we have created to be in the world, as the Parable of the Sower explains.[13] In the Parable of the Sower, Jesus tells a story about his words being the seeds of eternal life, but those seeds cannot take root within the person we have created to be in the world.

> Hear then the parable of the sower. When anyone hears the word and does not understand it, the evil one comes and snatches away what was sown in the heart; this is what was sown on the path. As for what was sown on rocky ground, this is the one who hears the word and immediately receives it with joy; yet such a person has no root, but endures only for a while, and when trouble or persecution arises on account of the word, that person immediately falls away. As for what was sown among thorns, this is the one who hears the word, but

the cares of the world and the lure of wealth choke the word, and it yields nothing. But as for what was sown on good soil, this is the one who hears the word and understands it, who indeed bears fruit and yields, in one case a hundredfold, in another sixty, and in another thirty.[14]

The beauty of Jesus' words cannot be seen from the perspective or level of consciousness we have acquired by being in the world, but only from that deeper life of who we were in God and who God was in us before the world began making us into its likeness. This is the deeper life we are trying to get back to through prayer at its deeper levels. The good soil in this parable is not the person that we have created to be in the world, but that deeper life of who we were in God and who God was in us before the world began making us into its likeness.

Becoming the good soil which is referred to in the Parable of the Sower is a matter of disidentifying with the person we have created to be in the world and identifying instead with who we are in God and who God is in us. But this deeper life to which Jesus calls us ultimately requires the death of the ego, the false self that we have created to be in the world.

To experience this deeper life to which Jesus calls his followers we need to see the lie of the false self we have created and to yearn for the deeper life to which Jesus calls us. Jesus' words to his disciples are the most beautiful words ever spoken, but their beauty cannot be seen from the perspective the world has given us. Thus, the spiritual life to which Jesus calls his followers is one of dying to the life we have created in the likeness of the world so that the deeper life might come forth.

Jesus' words to his disciples are living words meant to produce the divine fruit of mercy, forgiveness, and love within us. But those divine words cannot take root in the person created for the world, but only within that deeper life of who we were in God before the world began molding us into its likeness. Getting back to who we were in God before the world began molding us into its likeness is what the spiritual journey is all about. It is most essentially a death process: all those things we added to ourselves to become more than other people are shown to be lies to be discarded, so we can enter a life of following Jesus by being reduced to love.

The words of Jesus are constantly revealing our sin at ever deeper levels so we may become aware of God's mercy and forgiveness on ever deeper levels. This is what brings us into the deeper life to which Jesus calls his disciples. If we believe that our beliefs have made us righteous or sinless, we are at a very early stage in the spiritual journey. In fact, our religious beliefs do little more than inflate the ego or false self, which makes it impossible to love our enemy, and even our neighbor, in the same way we love ourselves.

Popular forms of Christianity tell us how to avoid the hard words of Jesus and go to heaven on the strength of what we must believe to have our sins forgiven. Jesus, however, never tells us what to believe, only how we should be if we are to bring his kingdom to earth. From our perspective in the world, a religious belief that gets our sins forgiven is ideal, since it offers a belief that allows us to avoid the spiritual journey and its transformation into the heavenly way to be that Jesus' words reveal. This does not mean that such churches present a false gospel, but rather that they present an elementary gospel. Where else would we begin but from the perspective the world has given us? Unfortunately, we can often get stuck in such early stages of the journey for years or even decades before we are drawn into the deeper life to which Jesus calls us.

---

1. Matthew 6:14-15.
2. Matthew 7:1-2.
3. Matthew 5:44.
4. Matthew 22:39.

5. Matthew 5:44.
6. Matthew 22:39.
7. John 15:7-10.
8. John 14:20.
9. John 14:26.
10. John 3:3.
11. 1 Timothy 1:15.
12. Smith, Adam. *An Inquiry into the Nature and Causes of the Wealth of Nations.* The Modern Library Edition. Random House. 1937, p. 14.
13. Matthew 13:1-23, Mark 4:1-20, and Luke 8:4-15.
14. Matthew 13:18-23.

CHAPTER 2
THE TWO LEVELS OF CONSCIOUSNESS AND THE DEEPER LIFE

There are two very distinct levels of human consciousness: One that connects us to the world and all the concerns the world demands that we address, and another, deeper level of consciousness, that connects us to God and to who we were in God and who God was in us before the world began making us into its likeness rather than God's likeness. Getting back to this deeper level of consciousness is what we practice in contemplative prayer.

The spiritual journey back to who we were in God and who God was in us is made necessary by the fact that Jesus' living words cannot take root in the person that we—and the world—have created to be successful in the world. As we have seen, Jesus tells his followers to forgive everyone,[1] judge no one,[2] and love even ones' enemies.[3] These are not things that can be done from the level of consciousness that the world has given us, so we try to find ways around the hard words of Jesus through our religious beliefs. One of today's more popular religious belief is that Jesus' death on the cross was payment for our sins, and with our sins paid for, we are now ready for heaven just as we are. As we have said, this is not necessarily a bad way to begin the spiritual journey back to God, so long as we don't get stuck there. The Salvation Gospel has great appeal to the person we have created to be in the world, and by the time we have made it through childhood, adolescence, and early adulthood most of us are the person the world and its ways have created. Thus, it is natural that we would begin the spiritual journey to which Jesus calls us by putting our faith in a belief that makes us better than other people, because being better than other people is the major point that we learn from being in the world.

As we have said, the world teaches us to strive to be better than our neighbors and our enemies through survival of the fittest, athletic competition, grades in school, a market economy based upon competition, and religious beliefs that make us better than others. Everything about the world puts us in competition with others, and those that win these competitions can come to see themselves as better than others. Jesus, however, tells us to love our neighbor in the same way we love ourselves.[4] This is the end of the spiritual journey to which Jesus calls us, but it requires an enormous transformation from the person we have created to be in the world to the person God had created before the world began making us into its likeness. Getting back to who we are in God and who God is in us is what the spiritual journey is all about. This is what we practice in prayer at its deeper levels.

Of course, prayer, for most of us is about petitioning God concerning our life in the world. The deeper levels of prayer, however, don't usually begin until we come to realize the lie of the false self that we have created to be in the world. Sadly, some never come to see that that self we create to be seen (by both ourselves and others) as more powerful, more beautiful, smarter, holier, etc., is just an illusion. We attempt to give ourselves the *appearance* of being better than other human beings. This is where we usually begin the spiritual journey, but there is a deeper life where the words of Jesus begin to come to life within us. Finding this deeper life is what the spiritual journey is all about.

The reason a deeper life is necessary for Jesus' words to come to life within us is because from the perspective the world has given us, we cannot see the beauty of Jesus' words. Loving our enemies[5] and not responding to violence with violence[6] make no sense from the level of consciousness that connects us to the world. To see the beauty of Jesus' words and to want those living words to come to life within us, we must find and practice a deeper life than the one we have created to be in the world. The more successful we become at developing a self that is good at adapting to the world's ways, the less we will be able to see the beauty of Jesus' words and the less we will want those living words to come to life within us.

Neither the Romans nor the Jewish leaders of Jesus' day could see the beauty of his words because they had created identities, or notions of themselves, that led them to believe they were better than other people. Religions often participate in this illusion by propagating beliefs that claim to make some people better in God's sight than other people, but the ultimate point of the gospel is to see ourselves in God and God in us, so we can understand that God is in everyone, and everyone deserves to be loved even when they are completely unaware of their being in God and God being in them.

Prayer at its deepest level is the practice of being in God and God being in us. This is the deepest level of our being, and getting back to that deepest level and learning to live out of who we are in God and who God is in us is what the transformation wrought by the spiritual journey is all about. It is not about becoming more than our neighbors and our enemies, but about becoming less, so we might become those empty vessels through whom Jesus' mercy, forgiveness, and love might pass to the world unobstructed by the judgments of the ego.

Do you remember the Parable of the Sower from the last

chapter? Jesus tells us that his words are the seeds of eternal life but for those seeds to produce the fulness of eternal life, they must take root in who we are in God rather than who we are in the world. Some of the sower's seeds fall upon the path that our lives in the world have created. That path is very much like the rocky ground that we have become in response to the world, which has hardened the person we have become by adapting to the world's ways. Likewise, the thorny ground, which represents "the cares of the world and the lure of wealth," chokes the word and makes it impossible for Jesus' words to take root and produce fruit. The words of Jesus to his disciples cannot take root in the person we have created to be in the world. Jesus' words, if they are to take root, require the rich soil of who we were in God and who God was in us before the world began making us into its likeness.

When speaking to his disciples, Jesus is seldom speaking to that self that they have created to be in the world. When speaking to his disciples he is usually speaking to that deeper life of who they are in God and who God is in them. This deeper life is what changes our perspective, for now we can see the beauty of Jesus' words. We begin to want those living words to come to life within us.

This deeper life that we can practice in contemplative prayer can provide us with a perspective very different from the perspective of our life in the world. As we have said, from the perspective of our life in the world, prayer is usually a matter of telling God of our needs in the world, but there is a deeper level of prayer and a deeper level of consciousness where we allow God to reveal to us the beauty of Jesus' words. This perspective, which allows us to see the beauty of Jesus' words, is the unitive level of consciousness that Jesus promises his disciples at the end of John's Gospel. "On that day you will know that I am in my Father, and you in me, and I in you."[7] This unitive consciousness of being in Jesus and Jesus being in us is what we practice in prayer at its deepest level.

The way we practice being in Jesus and Jesus being in us is through the Christian mystics' practice of silence. Silence is that level of consciousness that has no content. Unlike the level of consciousness that connects us to the world and which fills our consciousness with a constant flow of ideas and thoughts binding us to the world, Jesus' words to his followers are always speaking to who we are in God, and who God is in us, although followers of Jesus usually don't comprehend this until later in the spiritual journey. Their lives in the world have to be diminished sufficiently that they come to identify with and start operating out of that deeper life of who they are in God and who God is in them.

Of course, if we never spend time alone in the silence and stillness of who we were in God and who God was in us before the world remade us into its likeness, the words of Jesus will never take root, since they make little or no sense on the level of world-created consciousness. On that level, it makes no sense to forgive everyone,[8] judge no one,[9] and love even your enemy.[10] Jesus' words are not meant to make sense from the perspective the world has given us; Jesus' words are meant to transform us into beings capable of bringing Jesus' kingdom to earth.

Jesus ends the Parable of the Sower by telling us of the seed that was sown on good soil: "this is the one who hears the word and understands it, who indeed bears fruit and yields, in one case a hundredfold, in another sixty, and another thirty."[11] Our understanding of Jesus' heavenly words requires a heavenly perspective. Jesus' words to his disciples are not like the rest of the Bible. Jesus' words represent a later stage in the development of our species. Jesus is the alpha and omega of human history. He is the reason everything came into existence, and the end toward which human history is being divinely drawn.

The words of Jesus in the Bible make little sense when seen through the lens that the world has given us. It is only from the perspective of the deeper life that we can see the beauty of Jesus' words, because it is Jesus in us that allows us that beatific vision.

Much of the Bible is telling us how to be righteous in the world, but Jesus' words are telling us about a heavenly way to be that will bring Jesus' kingdom to earth. Of course, most people don't want that much heaven in their life, because it requires a radically different way to be than the way the world has taught us to be. The world teaches us to be better than our neighbors and our enemies. That is what righteousness is all about from the perspective the world has given us. But Jesus calls us to a deeper life, inviting us to see ourselves in our neighbors and loving them in the same way we love ourselves.[12]

This is the deeper life to which Jesus calls his followers, and the spiritual journey is all about getting us to that deeper life. The reason this deeper life requires a spiritual journey is because the words of Jesus can never take root within the person that we have created to be in the world, a person that just wants to be better off than our neighbors and our enemies. Much of religion appeals to the person we are in the world, since that is usually where we begin the spiritual journey, but the words of Jesus are always calling us to our deeper life, and that requires our disidentification with the ego that we have created. We love the self that we have created to be in the world, because we believer that we have created that self. But there is a deeper life that God had created before the world began molding us into its likeness. This is the true self that we are trying to get back to in the deepest levels of prayer.

The journey back to who we were in God and who God was in us is a journey of repentance and forgiveness for our participation in creating the false self that we and the world have created to be better than others. Seeing ourselves as better than other human beings is the great sin that prevents us from seeing the beauty of Jesus' words. It is also why Jesus' early disciples were generally lowly peasants rather than Roman citizens or Jewish leaders.

Discovering who we are in God, and who God is in us, is the end of the spiritual journey, but it ultimately requires the death of the ego—the false self. If we imagine ourselves to be in God and God to be in us at an early stage in the spiritual journey it will merely serve to inflate our egos and cause us to see ourselves as worth more than our neighbors and enemies, rather than those empty vessels, devoid of ego, allowing God's love, mercy, and forgiveness to pass to the world through us just as it had through Jesus.

If we operate out of the understanding the world has given us, we may claim to love Jesus, but the words of Jesus are too strange to be taken seriously by most who claim to be Christians. Thus, we love churches that love the Bible but avoid the hard words of Jesus. Mega churches and television Christianity give the people what they want, which is to avoid hell and gain heaven at the cheapest possible price. If you can throw in health and wealth as well that would be great, but such a gospel must avoid the hard words of Jesus, which tell a very different story.

The gospel that Jesus preached to his followers was one of a transformed life where Jesus' living words can come to life within them and ultimately allow them to forgive everyone,[13] judge no one,[14] and love even their enemies.[15] This perhaps best describes the gospel and the end of the spiritual journey to which Jesus calls us. It is not a gospel about our beliefs but about finding a deeper life in God rather than our life in the world.

> As you, Father, are in me and I am in you, may they also be in us, so that the world may believe that you have sent me. The glory that you have given me I have given them, so that they may be one as we are one, I in them and you in me, that they may become completely one, so that the world may know that you have sent me and have loved them even as you have loved me.[16]

Of course, this is not something that can happen early in the spiritual journey when we are still living out of the false self that we have created to be in the world. As we have said, if we try to realize unitive consciousness early in the journey it will tend to merely inflate the ego or false self. Indeed, the only gospel that the false self can love is one that benefits the false self, while the only self from which we can see the beauty of Jesus' words is that deeper life of who we were in God and who God was in us before the world began shaping us into its likeness in order to be better than our neighbors and enemies.

This deeper life to which Jesus calls us is what gives us the beauty of seeing ourselves in that other person and wanting to serve as the instrument through whom God's love, mercy, and forgiveness might pass to them without being hindered by our judgments, feelings, or beliefs. This is the deeper life, but it is one of becoming less rather than more than the person we are in the world. The spiritual journey is a descent into the unitive consciousness that Jesus promises his disciples at the end of John's Gospel. This unitive consciousness is the end of the spiritual journey, but it requires a radically different existence than the way the world has taught us to be.

---

1. Matthew 6:14-15.
2. Matthew 7:1-2.
3. Matthew 5:44.
4. Matthew 22:39; Mark 12:31.

5. Matthew 5:44.
6. Matthew 5:39.
7. John 14:20.
8. Matthew 6:14-15.
9. Matthew 7:1-2.
10. Matthew 5:44.
11. Matthew 13:23.
12. Matthew 22:39.
13. Matthew 6:14-15.
14. Matthew 7:1-2.
15. Matthew 5:44.
16. John 17:21-23.

CHAPTER 3

THE SPIRITUAL JOURNEY AND THE DEATH OF THE FALSE SELF

We usually begin the spiritual journey with epistemic truths or beliefs that we hold to be true, rather than revelations of deeper ontological ways of being. This became especially the case in the modern period of Western history, when epistemological truth came to be conceptualized after the mathematical model of truth as objective, certain, and precise. The scientific revolutions of the modern period prized mathematics as the ultimate form of human knowledge because of its apparent certainty, precision, and relative lack of varying philosophical perspectives that affected other areas of inquiry. The apparent success of this new mathematical physics had an enormous effect upon many aspects of the larger culture of the modern period, not the least of which was religion. The Protestant denominations that arose in the modern period prized beliefs that were logically consistent and precise, and the mysticism that was so prevalent within the ancient and medieval periods of the church was eliminated (except for perhaps the Quakers).

Ancient and Medieval mysticism spoke of a deeper level of consciousness than the empirical consciousness that connects us to the world of everyday affairs, and taught that this level of consciousness could be accessed through the prayer of silence or what came to be known as contemplation. Of course, this deeper level of consciousness was not easily accessed because it ultimately required a disidentification with the level of consciousness that connects us with the empirical world.

Of course, people can claim to have mystical experiences without being disconnected from the empirical world. Human consciousness and imagination can open us to a vast variety of experiences that are not always Divine. Fortunately, there is a litmus test to know if this deeper level of consciousness that we practice in the silence of prayer is Divine or of some other origin. The test is simply whether this deeper level of consciousness allows us to see the beauty of Jesus' words, which do not appear to be beautiful from the perspective the world has given us. For example, in the Gospels, Jesus has eight different teachings against the evil of money or wealth, yet the mind that connects us to the world tells us that a beautiful life is one of wealth and overcoming poverty. By contrast, Jesus tells us that poverty is the virtue, not wealth. So many of Jesus' teachings make no sense from the perspective the world has given us. Do we really think it is wise to refuse to respond to violence with violence,[1] and to respond in love[2] toward our enemies? From our perspective in the world, the words of Jesus make little or no sense, but on a deeper level of consciousness we can see the beauty of Jesus' words, and we want those living words to take root at the deepest core of our being.

Of course, this deeper level of consciousness that connects us to God rather than the world is not easily accessed, and if we attempt to access it too early in the spiritual journey the experience of the Divine will tend to inflate the ego and convince the false self that we are more than our neighbors and especially more than our enemies. The remedy to this evil of seeing ourselves as more than our neighbors and enemies is a spiritual journey which leads to the death of the false self we have created to cope with the world. This journey into the deeper life to which Jesus calls us is intended to reduce us to who we were in God and who God was in us before the world began making us into its likeness. This is the deeper life or unitive consciousness that Jesus reveals to his followers. He invites us to make that level of consciousness the dominant level of consciousness out of which we live our lives. "On that day you will know that I am in my Father, and you in me and I in you."[3] Jesus promises this unitive level of consciousness to his disciples because it is only from the perspective of being in God and God being in us that we can see the beauty of Jesus' words. Only then will those living words begin to take root at the deeper core of our being.

Jesus tells his disciples that if they stay on the journey to which he has called them that they can have his own level of consciousness and his own perspectives of being in God and God being in him. This is a very different perspective than the one we have acquired by being in the world. The world teaches us to see ourselves as very different entities than our neighbors and especially our enemies, but Jesus is trying to teach us how to see ourselves in our neighbors and even in our enemies. This level of consciousness that allows us to see ourselves in our neighbors and even in our enemies is the unitive consciousness of seeing ourselves in God and God in us. As we have said, however, if we try to access this deeper level of consciousness too early in the spiritual journey, while we are still operating out of the egoic level of consciousness, which we and the world have created to be in the world, our God experiences will tend to inflate the ego and have the opposite effect of causing us to see ourselves as more than our neighbors rather than less.

Again, God's ultimate purpose is that we might become those empty vessels through whom God's love, mercy, and forgiveness might pass to the world without interference from the judgments, opinions, and desires of the false self that we have created by being in the world. Jesus was that empty vessel through whom God's love passed to the world. This was the level of consciousness that Jesus revealed throughout the Gospels, and it is the level of consciousness to which Jesus calls his followers.

Again, if we attempt to access this unitive consciousness of being in God and God being in us too early in the spiritual journey it will tend to inflate the ego or false self, which wants to be like Jesus in terms of working miracles, healing the sick, and raising the dead, because the ego desires to be seen as something greater than other human beings. Jesus, on the other hand, was always revealing himself to be less than other human beings and no more than that empty vessel through whom his Father's love, mercy, and forgiveness might pass to the world.

This deeper life to which Jesus calls his followers is largely a matter of disidentifying with the ego that we have created to be in the world in order that our deeper life in God and God in us might come forth. Before the ego that we and the world have created begins to die, we don't want to become the empty vessels through whom God's love, mercy, and forgiveness might pass into the world without interference from the false self.

This emptying ourselves of ego is a large part of our spiritual descent into the deeper life to which Jesus calls us. Early in the spiritual journey, we want a God who saves the false self that we have created, not a God who desires us to be empty vessels passing through his love, mercy, and forgiveness to the world. Indeed, at the beginning of the spiritual journey we are content with beliefs that promise to secure a heavenly place in the afterlife that resembles our earthly happiness. But creating, through Jesus' words, the nature and character of our eternal life ultimately requires the eventual death of the ego that we have created to be in the world, the ego that just wants to be greater than our neighbors and our enemies.

Popular forms of Christianity appeal to the false self and offers beliefs that purport to make the false self better in God's sight than our neighbors and our enemies who lack such beliefs. Of course, Jesus never tells us what to *believe*, but rather how to *be* if we are to bring his kingdom to earth. Jesus' words to his followers, therefore, are not compatible with that level of consciousness we have developed by being in the world.

Who we are in God and who God is in at the deepest core of our being is the basis for our ultimate identity in God, which is the end of the spiritual journey. This deeper life, which is the end of the spiritual journey, requires a lifetime of allowing the person we have created to succeed in the world to die. That is the only way for our deeper life in God to come forth. The way the false self or ego dies is by our refusal to love the things that will make us appear to be more than other people. What feeds the ego are those worldly things that make us appear to be more than others. Wealth, power, prestige, physical beauty, strength, talent, and religious beliefs are the kinds of things that we identify with to assure us that we are better than our neighbors and especially better than our enemies.

The way the world keeps us from the deeper life to which Jesus calls us is by insisting that our life will be meaningful if we focus our love upon those things that make us appear to be more than other people. But Jesus tells us that our lives will be heavenly if we refuse to love the things that the world tells us to love, and instead focus our love on blessing others rather than ourselves. This is the great wisdom of heaven, but we only come fully into this wisdom through the death of the ego and the extinguishment of its desire to be more rather than less.

Eternal life is not on a pass/fail basis, but is determined by how seriously we take the words of Jesus, who tells us,

"You shall love the Lord your God with all your heart, and

with all of your soul, and with all of your mind." This is the greatest and first commandment. And the second is like it: "You shall love your neighbor as yourself."[4]

Divine love is something to give away and not something to receive; it is not meant to make you become more than other people. But in the early stages of the spiritual journey our religious beliefs and righteous behavior have the opposite effect: they increase the ego's desire to be more rather than less. Being loved by God is not the result of something we have done but the result of who God is. Of course, so long as the ego is what is directing our lives, we attribute God's love toward us as the result of something special within us, like our beliefs or righteous behavior. The end of the spiritual journey, however, is our recognition that what God ultimately desires is that God's mercy, forgiveness, and love might freely pass through us to the world, just as it had with Jesus.

Of course, this is the end of the transformative journey that lies at the base of the gospel, but this journey begins with the self that we have created to be in the world. As we have seen, our experiences throughout childhood, adolescence, and early adulthood create the person we become in the world. Most people begin the spiritual journey as that person they have created to be in the world. They take pride in the fact that they are better than other people because they have acquired more wealth, power, prestige, or righteousness than their neighbors.

When we first hear the call to a deeper life, it is that self which we have created to be in the world that hears and interprets that call. From the perspective the world has given us, we might imagine that God is going to do great things with our lives and make us into something more than our neighbors and our enemies. There are a lot of examples of this in the Old Testament, but Jesus represents a later development in the evolution of the world. Jesus is calling his followers to give themselves to the interests of others in order that Jesus' heavenly kingdom might come to earth. Following Jesus on this deeper level requires a deeper life than the one we have created to be in the world. The way we come into this deeper life is through repentance over Jesus' words and through prayer at its deeper levels.

From our perspective in the world, it makes no sense to forgive everyone,[5] judge no one,[6] and love even your enemies.[7] We can only see the beauty of Jesus' words from the perspective of the deeper life. Of course, the point of the spiritual journey is to ultimately identify with that deeper life and direct our love from the perspective of that deeper life. The way we practice this deeper life and eventually come to identify with it, rather than the life we have created to be in the world, is through prayer at its deepest level. When we pray out of the level of consciousness that connects us to the world, the self that we have created to be in the world uses words to inform God of the needs of the false self. When we pray out of that deeper life of who we were in God and who God was in us before the world began making us into its likeness, we pray out of silence and stillness to represent our willingness to allow God to do what God wants to do in our life. The way God does that is by revealing the beauty of Jesus' words, a revelation not conceivable by a worldly consciousness. From the perspective of the ego or false self, it makes no sense to love our enemies (or even our neighbors) in the same way we love ourselves. But when we can see ourselves in God and God in us, we can begin to identify as those angelic beings through whom God's love might freely flow to the world without being effected by the concerns of the ego.

This is the end of the spiritual journey and not the place from which we begin the spiritual journey. We may experience flashes of this deeper life early in the spiritual journey, but those experiences often have the unfortunate effect of inflating the false self. We see numerous examples of this with Jesus' own disciples, Peter being perhaps the most obvious example. He was used of God to bring truth forth only to have it inflate his ego, and he needed to be corrected by Jesus. In the sixteenth chapter of Matthew's Gospel, Jesus asks his disciples, "Who do people say the Son of Man is?"[8] To which different disciples give different answers. But Jesus asks again, "But who do you say that I am?" To which Peter responds, "You are the Messiah, the son of the living God."[9] To which Jesus responds.

> Blessed are you, Simon son of Jonah! For flesh and blood has not revealed this to you, but my Father in heaven. And I tell you, you are Peter, and on this rock I will build my church, and the gates of Hades will not prevail against it.[10]

Having said this about Peter, only three verses later Jesus begins to explain how "he must go to Jerusalem and undergo great suffering at the hands of the elders and chief priests and scribes, and be killed, and on the third day be raised."[11] To which Peter responds,

> "God forbid it, Lord! This must never happen to you." But he turned and said to Peter, "Get behind me Satan! You are a stumbling block to me; for you are setting your mind not on divine things but on human things."[12]

Early in the spiritual journey, our divine experiences tend to inflate the ego and cause us to see ourselves as more than others, as was the case with Peter, who needed to be corrected because he was still operating out of a consciousness that connected him to the world. The test to find out what level of consciousness we have acquired—if we are in the world or living the deeper life of being in God—is whether we can see the beauty of Jesus' words. If they seem to be nonsense, we are still burdened with the perspective the world has given us.

Loving your neighbor and even your enemy in the same way you love yourself is one test to see if you are operating out of ego or your deeper life in God. If that seems too extreme, we are not that far along in the spiritual journey. We should try the easier words of Jesus about what we should love and what we should not love.

God is love and desires that we become those empty vessels through whom his love, mercy, and forgiveness might pass to the world. What prevents that from happening is our love of the things that the world tells us to love. In our culture of advanced capitalism, wealth is the chief validation that we are better than others. Being better than other people is what our culture is all about, whether it be through wealth, power, prestige, beauty, talent, or religion. Jesus, however, does not call us to be better than other people, but rather to see ourselves in God and God in us. God wants his love, mercy, and forgiveness to flow through us to the world unrestricted by our own self-interest. That is who Jesus was and is calling us to be. This poverty of self to which Jesus calls his followers had no appeal to the Romans, who saw themselves as better than the rest of the world; nor did it have appeal to most of the Jewish leaders who saw themselves as better than other Jews. It did have appeal to the poor, however, who Jesus told were blessed with poverty so God's love might pass through them to the world unrestricted by self-interest.

This poverty out of which Jesus lived is the end of the spiritual journey, but for most of our lives it merely serves as the thing we constantly repent over to experience God's mercy and forgiveness. The end of the spiritual journey is that we become poor enough in spirit that God's mercy, forgiveness, and love might pass through us to the world, unrestricted by the self-interest that we have created to be in the world. This is the poverty of spirit that is the end of the spiritual journey to which Jesus calls us.

Jesus is always calling us to be poor in spirit, so we might live as Jesus lived with God's love passing through us to the world unrestricted by the interests of the self that we have created to be in the world, the false self that wants to be better off than others. This way of being better than other people may last for much of the spiritual journey, and for some it is the only motivation that their lives will ever know. If we pay attention to the words of Jesus, however, we eventually come to see that we are not capable of obeying Jesus from the level of consciousness we have acquired by being in the world. The most we can do from that level of consciousness is to repent over Jesus' words, but even so, it is a very important point in the spiritual journey, since it is only by receiving much mercy and forgiveness in response to our repentance that we begin to become like our heavenly Father and Jesus in terms of mercy and forgiveness.

What can keep us from this deeper place in the journey is the belief that we have already received sufficient mercy and forgiveness through our professed beliefs in the Nicene Creed, the Salvation Gospel, or whatever other beliefs that we purport to have made us better than those without such beliefs. This is as far as many believers wish to go. Others may desire to go further in the spiritual journey and seek a righteousness that is rooted in more than their beliefs, but early attempts at righteousness almost always turn into their ego's attempt to appear greater than other egos.

Much of religion applauds our wanting to be better than other human beings, but the end of the spiritual journey is ultimately about becoming less, so that God's love might pass through us to the world unrestricted by self-interest, just as Jesus had served as that empty vessel through whom God poured his mercy, forgiveness, and love to the world. Jesus was so much less than the rest of us that he was indistinguishable from God himself.

Of course, the popular gospel does not address this deeper life of who we are in God and who God is in us, but instead addresses who we have created to be in the world. From the perspective of the ego, self-interest is our primary interest and does not extend very far beyond close relatives and friends. To get to the place where our only interest is to become God's empty vessels through whom God might transform the world, a deeper life is required. But we only reach this deeper life through the death of the life we have created to be in the world. Because death is involved in this transformative process it is no wonder that the spiritual journey takes a lifetime and is often aided by a natural decline of the life we have created to be in the world. Aging and handicaps disable our ability to be better than others in the world and are the blessings that can cause us to seek a deeper life in God.

The spiritual journey is a lifelong matter of disidentifying with the self that we have created to be in the world and instead identifying with our deeper life in God. We learn to disconnect from the level of consciousness that connects us to the world. Its endless flow of one idea after another in a rapid sequence makes us oblivious to the very consciousness on which these ideas rest. We have to practice the deeper life through the prayer of silence. Consciousness itself is the path to awareness of the deeper life, but it must be practiced if it is to become the dominant level of consciousness out of which we live our lives. The deeper level of consciousness is necessary to create the life to which Jesus calls us, because it is only from the deeper perspective that we can see the beauty of Jesus' words and want those living words to come to life within us.

From the level of consciousness that connects us to the world, it makes no sense to love our enemies, but if we practice the deeper life enough, we can see how beautiful and freeing it is to forgive everyone,[13] judge no one,[14] and love even our enemies.[15] Of course, this is very different from popular interpretations of the gospel, which address the false self that we have created to be in the world. The egoic self does what it believes is in its interest, so popular religion offers beliefs that exonerate our sins, free us from hell, and make us ready for heaven on the strength of our beliefs alone.

The Nicene Creed was the first attempt at faith as belief, ignoring the radically different way that Jesus had taught his disciples to be. Today's popular belief, and a detour around the hard words of Jesus, is the Salvation Gospel, which claims that our belief that Jesus' death on the Cross was payment for our sins, and our sins were the only thing that were keeping us from the fullness of eternal life in God.

Again, this is not to say that the Salvation Gospel is a false gospel, but only that it is an elementary gospel. Where else would we begin than with a gospel that appeals to the false self because it offers the greatest reward at the cheapest price? But the life that Jesus calls us to requires the death of that false self that we and the world have created to be in the world. If we believe that our beliefs are what make us better than other people in God's sight, the ego is all for endorsing Christianity, but the words of Jesus are another matter. Jesus' words are always trying to reduce us to no more than who we are in God and who God is in us.

Unlike our beliefs, Jesus' words are not intended to make us more than other people, but less. That is because the words of Jesus cannot take root in the worldly ego we have created. Becoming a follower of Jesus may initially appear to add something to our life in the world, and early in the spiritual journey our beliefs and attempts at righteousness may make us appear to be more than other people, but if we stay on the journey and begin to pay attention to Jesus' words, we begin to see that the beauty of those words can only be seen from that deeper perspective of who we are in God and who God is in us.

Likewise, if Jesus' living words are to come to life within us, those living words can only take root in our deeper life in God rather than who we are in the world. Practicing that deeper life of prayer and learning to live out of that deeper life is what the spiritual journey is all about.

This is what the great Christian mystics and saints have always understood, but the Protestant reformations of the modern period eliminated the mystics and saints who knew that eternal life was not attained on a pass/fail criterion based upon mere belief. What the mystics and saints knew was that the deeper, transformed life comes about through a journey that involves the progressive death of the egoic, false self, so our deeper life in God might come forth. Again, mystics and saints are not more than other people, but less. The hard words of Jesus that we find in the Sermon on the Mount, the parables of Jesus, and the Farewell Discourse at the end of John's Gospel[16] tell of a radically different way to be in the world than the way our culture at a particular point in human history has taught us to be.

This deeper life requires a level of consciousness very different from the one the world has given us. To get to the level of consciousness where the world no longer owns our minds and dominates us with an endless barrage of thought after thought, we must practice that deeper level of consciousness that connects us to who we are in God and who God is in us. If we practice this deeper level of consciousness enough that it becomes our dominant level of consciousness, we gain the perspective from which we can see the beauty of Jesus words, which cannot be seen from the perspective the world has given us.

This deeper level of consciousness that gives us access to the beauty of Jesus' words must be practiced to become dominant. Furthermore, there are multiple dangers in exploring alternative levels of consciousness. I think the best guide in exploring this deeper level of consciousness is found in the words of Jesus. But Jesus' words need to be explained, and that is the job of the Holy Spirit. "But the Advocate, the Holy Spirit, whom the Father will send in my name, will teach you everything, and remind you of all that I have said to you."[17] In order to be taught the words of Jesus by the Holy Spirit, a new mind is required since Jesus' words make little sense from the mind formed by the cultural and historic world of our time. We begin to acquire this new mind through the prayer of silence, since it is neither fuller nor richer than the mind that we have acquired by being in the cultural and historical world of our time in human history. That new mind will be less, since it is our original state of mind before the world began making us into its likeness.

The process of becoming less rather than more is what the spiritual journey is all about. We all began with a mind without content except for the fact that we knew that we were in God and God was in us. Our emersion into the world, however, forced us to make sense of our experiences in ways that are appropriate to the cultural and historical standards of our time.

As we have seen, in today's world we are taught to be better than other human beings through athletic competition, grades in school, survival of the fittest, a competitive market economy, and religious beliefs that make us better in God's sight than people without our beliefs. In the culture of Jesus' day, the popular paths to become better than other individuals were either to be a Roman citizen or a Jewish leader. It is not coincidental that most who were either Roman citizens or Jewish leaders did not become followers of Jesus, since Jesus was teaching his followers how to be less than, rather than more than other individuals. By the time Jesus had reached the age of thirty, whatever false self or ego that he had developed through his childhood, adolescence, and early adulthood had died, and he had become that empty vessel through whom God's mercy, forgiveness, and love might pass to the world.

Jesus' teachings are always about this deeper life and how this deeper life only comes forth through the death of the false self created to be in the world. If Jesus' living words are to take root within us and make us into his disciples, a deeper life than the life of the ego is required. How much death to the ego we experience goes a long way in determining how much transformation into Jesus' likeness we are willing to experience.

Of course, this is the end of the spiritual journey and not where we begin. In the early stages of the journey, we are living out of the egoic false self that we have created to be in the world, rather than our deeper life in God and God in us. Getting to that deeper life is what the spiritual journey is all about. From the perspective of the ego, the better life is one that makes us better than our neighbors and our enemies, while the life that Jesus lived was a life devoid of ego that he might be that empty vessel through whom God's mercy, forgiveness, and love might freely flow to the world.

Getting to that place where we no longer identify with the self that the ego creates us to be in the world, and to be in the world in a better state than our neighbors and our enemies, is what the spiritual journey is all about. How far we progress on that journey is what determines where we begin eternal life. Of course, this is not the popular gospel, which tells us that we can have the fullness of eternal life simply by having the right belief, which makes us better than other people.

Jesus' words, however, are always calling us to be less rather than more than our neighbors and our enemies. By the time Jesus began his public ministry, he had no ego or false self, or to put it in another way, Jesus' self-interest was in God and God was in his self-interest. That is the deeper life to which Jesus calls his followers as well, but it takes a lifetime to get to that place since it requires a spiritual journey that involves the death of the false self that we have created to be in the world, and to be in a better state than our neighbors and our enemies.

I know that Christianity, especially from the perspective of the early stages of the spiritual journey, sees Jesus as a superhero with the powers to do whatever he wants, but that is the naïve imagination of the false self which we have created to be in the world. Jesus, in a mere thirty years, had completed the spiritual journey back to who he was in God and who God was in him before the world began trying to make him into its likeness. This is the end of the spiritual journey and why Jesus tells us, "Unless you become as little children you will never enter the kingdom of heaven."[18]

This process of becoming less rather than more is what the spiritual journey is all about. It takes us through various stages of righteousness which may begin with little more than religious beliefs and a desire to be righteous by keeping God's commandments, but eventually, if we stay on the journey, we come to see that Jesus is calling us to a level of being that cannot be realized by the self we have created to be in the world, and a deeper life is required if Jesus words are to come to life within us.

It should not be surprising that it takes years for us to even be willing to attempt this deeper life, since the death of the ego often means the end of the only life we have known. Thus, this deeper life is not one that we see Christians fighting over to achieve. Likewise, it is not surprising that the Christianity of the modern Protestant period eliminated both mystics and saints and reduced the gospel to be about our beliefs and our righteousness, rather than our deeper life in God and God in us that Jesus describes at the end of John's Gospel.[19]

The end of the spiritual journey is not about getting rid of our sins by having the right beliefs, but about coming to love the things Jesus tells us to love and not loving the things that Jesus tells us not to love. It is not about getting rid of our sins, but about getting rid of the cause of our sin, which is that we love the things the world tells us to love rather than the things Jesus tells us to love.

---

1. Matthew 5:39.
2. Matthew 5:44.
3. John 14:20.
4. Matthew 22:37-39.
5. Matthew 6:14.
6. Matthew 7:1-2.
7. Matthew 5:44.
8. Matthew 16:13.
9. Matthew 16:16.
10. Matthew 16:17-18.
11. Matthew 16:21.
12. Matthew 16:22-23.
13. Matthew 6:14-15.
14. Matthew 7:1-2.
15. Matthew 5:44.
16. John 14-17.
17. John 14:26.
18. Matthew 18:3.
19. John 14-17.

CHAPTER 4
THE TWO LOVES AND THE DEEPER LIFE

Love is our strongest affection, but it comes in two distinct forms. In its human form, we love or have affection for those things that we can acquire to make our lives better than other people's lives. Since most people have little sense of what is ultimately good, we end up having affection for whatever our culture at a particular point in human history says is desirable, and we are judged by how well we fare at achieving these goods in comparison to our neighbors. This is the love that develops out of scarcity and competition over resources. It is what causes us to develop skills or talents that make us better than others at getting a job, getting a spouse, a better place on the team, or a better seat on the plane.

There is, however, another *divine* form of love. It is the affection we can develop for giving ourselves away in acts of love. This is the love that lies at the heart of the gospel. God is love but God needs nothing so what God loves is to give love away to others to make them more loving for having been loved, more merciful for having received mercy, and more forgiving for having been forgiven much. If you cannot identify with such a life and think you have not been loved greatly and experienced great mercy or forgiveness, the reason is that you have not been paying attention to the words of Jesus. Jesus' words reveal the great depth of our sin, and only time alone in God's presence and Jesus' words can reveal that God's mercy, forgiveness, and love are always deeper than our sin. This is the transformative experience that reduces us to love, if we practice it enough. What keeps us from such a transformative experience is the belief that our sins have been forgiven because of our beliefs, and we are ready for heaven just as we are.

The nature and character of our eternal life, however, is not determined by our beliefs, but by the nature of our love. We may begin the spiritual life with religious beliefs that we claim make us better than other people, but Jesus' words are meant to reduce us to love, mercy, and forgiveness, by seeing the great depth of our sin, leading us to realize that God's mercy, forgiveness, and love are always deeper still.

Consider the fact that Jesus tells us to "Give to everyone who begs from you, and do not refuse anyone who wants to borrow from you."[1] Does anyone live like that? The words of Jesus are intended to reveal that we are not yet transformed into that deeper life in God to which Jesus calls us. Repentance over the fact that we do not love our neighbor, let alone our enemy, in the same way we love ourselves should open us to a constant flow of God's transformative mercy and forgiveness. Of course, if we are still at the early stages of the spiritual journey, we cling to religious beliefs that purport to make us righteous by Jesus having paid for our sins, but that simply makes us forgiven and not forgiving. God is forgiving and forgives our sins, but God does not forgive unforgiveness. That is our responsibility, and represents a deeper stage in the spiritual journey.

> For if you forgive others their trespasses, your heavenly Father

will forgive you; but if you do not forgive others, neither will your Father forgive your trespasses.[2]

The experience of being forgiven is intended to make us forgive others. If the experience of being forgiven has not made us into forgiving beings, we need to experience forgiveness at deeper and deeper levels. The ultimate end of the gospel is for us to become Jesus' mercy, forgiveness, and love to the world, and therein bring his kingdom to earth. We do not accomplish this end through our beliefs and righteous behavior, but by paying attention to Jesus' words and therein seeing our sin at ever deeper levels. We are only made merciful and forgiving by having received mercy and forgiveness, and that is why Jesus' words reveal our sin at ever deeper levels. Our own experience of mercy and forgiveness is felt at ever deeper levels, and therein are we transformed into his merciful and forgiving likeness.

The false self that we have created to be in the world can experience righteousness through our right beliefs. That is as far as it can go. But there is a deeper life in God: we can become the instruments of God's love, mercy, and forgiveness in the world. The death of the false self is the path to our transformation into Jesus' likeness. Jesus' words do not tell us what to believe so we can be better than other human beings in God's sight. Instead, Jesus' words reveal our sin at ever greater depths, that we might experience God's mercy and forgiveness at ever greater depths. Righteousness is certainly a stage in the spiritual journey, but it is an early stage and is eclipsed by mercy, forgiveness, and love—if we stay on the journey into the fullness of life to which Jesus calls us.

Early in the spiritual journey, however, it is easy to get stuck in righteousness because of our beliefs and righteous behavior, which we think make us better than other people. This is the love of the world, which tells us to love those things which make us better than other people. This love is very different from the divine love to which Jesus calls us. The affection that the world tells us to develop is a love for those things that make us better at acquiring things like pleasure, security, power, esteem, or survival. This love that we develop by being in the world attaches itself to those things that make us appear to be more than our neighbor and especially more than our enemies. But there is a deeper love than the love that the world has given us. It cannot be experienced from the level of consciousness which we have developed by being in the world. This deeper love is the angelic love that rests at the core of our being and desires nothing more than to be the vessel through whom God's mercy, forgiveness, and love might pass to the world. The false self or ego that we create to be in the world is not capable of this level of love. Of course, the false self can act mercifully and can be forgiving and loving. But that is not God's love passing through us to the world. Rather, it is an attempt by the false self to act like Jesus, rather than being that empty vessel through whom Jesus might live again within us. This is the unitive consciousness that Jesus promises to his disciples, as described in John's Gospel:

> On that day you will know that I am in my Father, and you in me, and I in you. They who have my commandments and keep them are those who love me; and those who love me will be loved by my Father, and I will love them and reveal myself to them.[3]

Unitive consciousness, or our conscious awareness of being in God and God being in us, is what the great saints and Christian mystics have practiced throughout the history of Christianity. What we see in the lives of those who have best followed Jesus over the last two thousand years is that their lives revealed a progressive decline in self-interest. The self that we and the world have created to be in the world has been taught to do everything out of self-interest. Sure, we have also learned to act unselfishly in order to be thought of as kinder than our neighbor, but for most of us such actions are still ego-driven and come from a desire to be more than others.

The deeper level of consciousness that connects us to God rather than the world must be practiced enough that it eventually becomes the dominant level of consciousness out of which we operate. This is the end of the spiritual journey as revealed through the life and death of Jesus. Jesus had probably developed an ego by being in the world, but by the age of thirty he had completed the spiritual journey and was no longer under the control of the world that rules us through self-interest. Loving those things that make us appear to be more than other human beings is the sin of the world, and the only way we escape that sin is by allowing the false self to die. This is the deeper life that Jesus lived and to which he calls his followers. What makes it so different is that it is from this perspective and this perspective alone that we can see how beautiful it is to forgive everyone,[4] judge no one,[5] and love even our enemies.[6]

This is what the great Christian saints and mystics understood. When we identify with this deeper life of our being in God and God being in us, the ego begins to die through our lack of attention to its demands. In contrast to the world, which tells us that more is better, Jesus tells us that the deeper life involves a spirit of poverty,[7] of becoming empty vessels through whom Jesus might live again and bring his transformative mercy, forgiveness, and love to the world. It is not without meaning that Jesus tells us in the first beatitude of the Sermon on the Mount that poverty is our greatest virtue. That is hard to see from early stages in the spiritual journey where we are still living out of the self that we have created to be in the world. The false self always desires to be more rather than less, but the deeper life is about decreasing the ego's control over our life until eventually we are no more than empty vessels through whom God may pour his mercy, forgiveness, and love to the world.

Being reduced to divine love is the end of the spiritual journey and poverty is the primary virtue we need to develop to get there. The opposite of poverty is wealth. Jesus has numerous teachings against wealth or money.

> Do not store up for yourself treasure on earth, where moth and rust consume, and where thieves break in and steal; but store up for yourself treasure in heaven, where neither moth nor rust consume and where thieves do not break in and steal. For where your treasure is, there your heart will be also.[8]

The world teaches us to be better than our neighbors and our enemies, and in the historical and cultural world of our time wealth or money is the major way people achieve that better status. But Jesus tells us that is an illusion. It is what keeps us from the deeper life to which Jesus calls us. The deeper life to which Jesus calls us is the poverty of who we were in God and who God was in us before the world began making us into its likeness.

The spiritual journey to which Jesus calls his followers ultimately requires us to get back to that deeper life of who we were in God and who God was in us before the world began making us into its likeness in order to be more than our neighbors and our enemies. Jesus is always calling his followers to be less rather than more. As we have seen, this was why Jesus tells Nicodemus early in John's Gospel that we must be "born from above..."[9] The spiritual journey is the way back to who we were in God and who God was in us before the world began making us into its likeness.

Of course, this is not the popular gospel. To be popular and embraced by many people, the gospel must appeal to the false self that we have created to be in the world, since that is the place where we most often begin the spiritual journey. The Salvation Gospel, like the Nicene Creed, is not a false gospel, but simply the place from which most of us begin the spiritual journey. How far we go in the spiritual journey is a matter of how much we disidentify with the false self that we have created to be in the world, how much we allow ourselves to be reduced to those empty vessels through whom Jesus might live again. This requires the ultimate poverty to which Jesus has been calling his followers for the last two thousand years. This poverty, which is the end of the spiritual journey, requires a lifetime of dying to the desires of the ego. The ego must die before we can experience unitive consciousness, because if we start believing that God is in us and we are in God too early in the spiritual journey, before the ego has even begun to die, the belief that God is in us will tend to inflate the ego and cause us to see ourselves as more than other human beings rather than less. If we wish to ascend into God's kingdom, we must descend into the emptiness that Jesus so perfectly revealed.

When we view Jesus' life from the perspective that the world has given us, we see him as greater than other men because of his ability to heal the sick and work miracles. But that ability of Jesus came through the fact that he was that ultimate empty vessel through whom God's mercy, forgiveness, and love might flow to the world, unobstructed by the cultural opinions and beliefs of the false self that we are all forced to develop to be in the world.

Early in the spiritual journey we operate almost exclusively out of ego or the false self that we have created to be in the world, and not out of the deeper life to which Jesus calls his followers. If we are to become the branches to Jesus' vine,[10] the false self must die, and the self that we operate out of must become who we were in God and who God was in us before the world began making us into its likeness. This is what it means to "love the Lord your God with all your heart, and with all your soul, and with all your mind."[11] Loving God with all our heart, soul, and mind leaves nothing left over from which to love our own independent self, which we take pride in believing we ourselves have created in order to be better than our neighbors and our enemies. This is the illusion that the spiritual journey is intended to destroy.

Jesus is always calling his followers to that deeper life of being in God and God being in them, just as Jesus was in God and God was in Jesus. This deeper life must be the ultimate end of the spiritual journey because the words of Jesus cannot take root in the person we have created to be in the world. From the perspective of our being in the world, it makes no sense to love others in the same way we love ourselves[12] or to refuse to respond to violence with violence.[13] There is, however, a deeper life from whose perspective we can experience the beauty of Jesus' words and experience the truth of those living words coming to life within us. His words cannot come to life within the false self, since they are radically opposed to the false self's agenda, which is to make itself appear to be more than other people, rather than less than other people, so that God's mercy, forgiveness, and love might freely pour through us to the world.

Of course, from the perspective of our life in the world, we can also act mercifully and forgiving. But early in the spiritual journey that is usually an act of the false self rather than God's love passing through us unobstructed by the ego and its judgments concerning who are worthy of God's love and who are not worthy. Jesus tells us that he is the vine, and we are the branches.

> I am the true vine, and my Father is the vinegrower. He removes every branch in me that bears no fruit. Every branch in me that bears fruit he prunes to make it bear more fruit.

> You have already been cleansed by the word that I have spoken to you. Abide in me as I abide in you. Just as the branch cannot bear fruit by itself unless it abides in the vine, neither can you unless you abide in me. I am the vine and you are the branches. Those who abide in me and I in them bear much fruit because apart from me you can do nothing.[14]

This is the deeper life that must be practiced if it is to become the dominant level of consciousness out of which we live our lives. Practicing this deeper level of consciousness where we practice being in God and God being in us is prayer at its deepest level, and it is only from this deeper level of consciousness that we can see the beauty of Jesus words and want those living words to take root at the deepest core of our being.

Before this deeper level of consciousness becomes the level of consciousness out of which we live our lives, we can act like we love our enemies, but it is an act of the false self seeking praise from others, rather than God's love passing through us to the world. Only the deeper life of who we are in God and who God is in us is can transform us into the empty vessels through whom God's mercy, forgiveness, and love passes into the world.

Of course, our earliest experiences of this deeper life tend to occur long before the death of the false self. Such experiences often tend to inflate the ego, giving us the idea that we are more than other people. But the ultimate end of the gospel is to become less—to be no more than empty vessels through whom God can direct his love, mercy, and forgiveness to the world.

We may begin the spiritual journey by believing that our acceptance of Jesus' atonement has made us righteous, but the end of the journey is to have Jesus' living words come to life within us. Unfortunately, Jesus' divine words are not compatible with the self that we have created to be in the world. In fact, we cannot even see the beauty of Jesus' words from the perspective the world has given us. Getting back to who we were in God and who God was in us, before the world began making us into its likeness, ultimately requires the death of the ego or false self that we have created to be in the world, the false self that seeks to be better than our neighbors and our enemies, rather than transform us into an empty vessel devoid of ego, just like Jesus.

There is a deeper life than the life we have created for ourselves to be in the world. That deeper life is the life that God had created before the world took hold of us and began making us into its likeness. Getting back to this deeper life is what the spiritual journey is all about, but the journey almost always begins with the false self.

Popular forms of Christianity appeal to the false self that we have created to be in the world and offer salvation for that false self in exchange for belief. But there is that deeper life that Jesus reveals. Given the human condition, it is hard to imagine the spiritual journey beginning anywhere but in the false self. Jesus himself experienced this universal temptation to be more than other human beings, turning away from who he was in God and who God was in him. By the age of thirty, however, Jesus had completed the spiritual journey and had become no more than who he was in God and who God was in him. He resisted the temptation to be more than other men and became that empty vessel through whom God's love flows into humanity without interference from that self which saw itself as more than other human beings. Jesus resisted the temptation to which the rest of us so easily succumb, because we are not at the end of our journeys into the deeper life to which Jesus calls us.

> The tempter came and said to him, "If you are the Son of God, command these stones to become loaves of bread." But he answered, "It is written, 'One does not live by bread

alone, but by every word that comes from the mouth of God.'"

Then the devil took him to the holy city and placed him on the pinnacle of the temple, saying to him, "If you are the son of God, throw yourself down, for it is written,

'He will command his angels concerning you' and 'On their hands they will bear you up, so that you will not dash your foot against a stone.'"

Jesus said to him, "Again it is written, 'Do not put the Lord your God to the test.'"

Again, the devil took him to a very high mountain and showed him all the kingdoms of the world and their splendor; and said to him, "All these I will give you, if you will fall down and worship me." Jesus said to him, "Away with you, Satan! For it is written, 'Worship the Lord your God and serve only him.'"[15]

These three temptations are the temptations the world always puts before the false self that we have developed by being in the world. Promises of power, esteem, and wealth are the things that make one individual appear to be more than others, but Jesus is always calling his followers to be less than others so God's mercy, forgiveness, and love might flow through them to the world, unrestricted by the ego's self-interest.

This revelation of Jesus being tempted to become more than other men reveals that by the time Jesus had reached thirty years of age whatever false self that had developed throughout his childhood, adolescence, and early adulthood had died. Jesus had begun to reveal God's ultimate revelation: a human being who was in God as God was in him, without any interference from an ego that strives to see itself as more than other men. From the perspective of our own egos, we may see Jesus as more than other human beings, but in fact Jesus was less than other human being. He was perfectly devoid of ego so his Father's love, mercy, and forgiveness might flow unrestricted through him to the world.

The life that Jesus lived—being in God and God being in him—is also the deeper life to which Jesus calls his followers. Indeed, it is only this deeper life in God and God in us that can give root to Jesus' words, since from the perspective of the ego, the words of Jesus make no sense. The ego sometimes acts as if it loves its neighbor (or even its enemy) in the same way it loves itself, but in the early stages of the spiritual journey that is most often the ego trying to appear to be better than other people. Ultimately, the deeper life of being in God and God being in us only comes forth through the progressive death of the ego.

---

1. Matthew 5:42.
2. Matthew 6:14-15.
3. John 14:20-21.
4. Matthew 6:14-15.
5. Matthew 7:1-2.
6. Matthew 5:44.
7. Matthew 5:3.
8. Matthew 6:19-21.
9. John 3:3.
10. John 15:1-5.
11. Matthew 22:37.
12. Matthew 22:39.
13. Matthew 5:39.
14. John 15:1–5.
15. Matthew 4:3–10.

CHAPTER 5
OUR BELIEFS AND RIGHTEOUSNESS VERSUS THE DEEPER LIFE

Our beliefs usually represent our initial commitment to the spiritual journey. As we have seen, it is natural that our spiritual journey would begin with beliefs, since from the ego's perspective in the world the best spiritual beliefs offer the greatest reward at the cheapest price. Gaining heaven at the price of a belief is certainly attractive, whether the belief be the Nicene Creed, the Salvation Gospel, or any other belief that makes us better than the rest of God's creation, since early in the spiritual journey we operate almost entirely out of the perspective of the false self or ego that we have created throughout childhood, adolescence, and early adulthood. From the perspective of that ego, which has taught us to make ourselves better than other people, the idea of gaining heaven and avoiding hell at the cost of a belief is certainly attractive.

Of course, the nature of the spiritual journey is ultimately about the death of the ego so our deeper life in God might come forth. Early in the spiritual journey, however, there is little understanding of the distinction between the ego and the deeper life to which Jesus is always calling us. At the early stages of the journey, we are largely unconscious of any such distinction and want our beliefs to be sufficient to assure us of God's love. We read the Bible and act righteously to support our delusion that our beliefs have made us better than other people. But at the same time, we work to avoid the words of Jesus, which constantly call us to be less than other people, to see our sin at ever greater depths. We may have beliefs that Jesus has paid for our sins, but Jesus says that God does not forgive our unforgiveness.

> For if you forgive others their trespasses, your heavenly Father will also forgive yours; but if you do not forgive others, neither will your Father forgive your trespasses.[1]

God does not forgive unforgiveness. The spiritual journey may begin with our beliefs about God's forgiveness being a response to our beliefs, but the words of Jesus are always speaking about our deeper life in God. Of course, when we begin the spiritual journey, we have little or no idea of the deeper life, or of how the spiritual journey transforms us into Jesus' likeness. The progression of the Christian life is one of transformation from the person that we and the world have created to be in the world, to the person that God had created before the world took hold of us and began making us into God's likeness.

This transformation may begin with a belief that proports to make us righteous, but the end toward which our journey always moves is found in the words of Jesus, and they are always at odds with our righteousness. That is because unlike beliefs that purport to make us righteous, Jesus' words are always pointing at the ever-deeper level of our sin in the hope of bringing us to repentance and leading us to ever greater experiences of God's mercy and forgiveness. This is the only way to the deeper life to which Jesus calls us. It may begin with a belief that makes us righteous, but the spiritual journey of transformation always moves beyond our righteousness toward the words of Jesus, which reveal our sin at ever deeper levels.

The words of Jesus are living words meant to come to life within us, but they cannot come to life within the egoic self that we have created to be in the world. The beauty of Jesus' words has little or no appeal to the ego, but speaks to that deeper life of who we are in God and who God is in us. The ego may want to be a follower of Jesus and be a healer or miracle worker, but not a person who has undergone a complete transformation, who gives himself away to others in acts of mercy, forgiveness, and love, just like Jesus. This is the deeper life to which Jesus' words are always calling us. The two things that can keep us from this deeper life to which Jesus calls us is getting stuck in our beliefs and ignoring the words of Jesus that call us to the unitive consciousness of being in God and God being in us.

Being in another and another being in us makes no sense to the ego. Throughout our childhood, adolescence, and early adulthood, we have developed a notion of self that is independent of others and puts us at odds with them as we compete for the scarce resources that the world tells us will make us better than our neighbors and especially better than our enemies. This self, produced by our culture at a particular time and place in human history, is totally alien to the idea that Jesus offers of being in another and another being in us.

The ego self that we develop to be in the world sees itself as a separate subject distinct from the objects that surround us. Early in the spiritual journey to which Jesus calls us, we operate almost exclusively out of the ego that creates the false self. Jesus, however, tells us of a deeper life of being in Jesus and Jesus being in us. This is the deeper life to which Jesus calls us, but there is a huge price to pay for this union. Jesus does not join us as a junior partner, but only under the condition that the ego has been sufficiently overcome. If we are still operating primarily out of the ego, the idea of God being in us and our being in God will tend to inflate the ego, which will try to convince us that we are justified in seeing ourselves as more than other people rather than less. This is not the ultimate poverty to which Jesus calls his followers. The end toward which the spiritual journey proceeds is the ultimate poverty of being able to function without an ego, of returning to who we were in God and who God was in us before the world insisted that we develop an ego to function according to the world's ways.

Of course, we can *imagine* that Jesus is in us and we are in Jesus, but if the ego is still the level of consciousness out of which we direct our lives, we will believe that Jesus' unitive consciousness makes us more than other people rather than less.

> On that day many will say to me, "Lord, Lord, did we not prophesy in your name, and cast out demons in your name, and do many deeds of power in your name?" Then I will declare to them, "I never knew you; go away from me, you evildoer."[2]

From the perspective of the ego that we have created to be in the world, we imagine that God must be the ultimate ego—the self that is the greatest of all selves and worthy of adoration and worship. But the God that Jesus reveals is a Father God who gives himself away to his creation without self-concern, and his Son, like his Father God, gives himself away to his Father's creation, because divine love is not a matter of acquiring the things we love, but of giving ourselves away to God's creation by becoming the vessels of God's mercy, forgiveness, and love to the world.

In the early stages of the journey, we are still operating out of the ego rather than our deeper life in God. Thus, we wish to be used by God not as empty vessels through whom God might pour his love to the world, but as special beings capable of miracles and supernatural powers, distinguishing us (or rather, our false selves) as more than others rather than less. Jesus was able to do miracles because by the time he began his public ministry he had completed the spiritual journey and was devoid of ego, just like his heavenly Father was devoid of ego.

Of course, we imagine that God must be the supreme ego because that is who we would be if we were God, the creator and maintainer of the universe. But a triune God, as Father, Son, and Spirit, are constantly giving themselves away to one another and their creation. That is the ultimate nature of the Divine, and it is beyond the imagination of the mind that the world has given us. Fortunately, there is a level of consciousness that does give us access to the Divine and allows us to see the beauty of Jesus' words, but it must be practiced if it is to become the dominant level of consciousness out of which we live our lives. The way we practice this deeper life is through our disidentification with the separate self or ego that we have created to be in the world, and our practice of identifying with our deepest level of being in God and God being in us.

Prayer, as silence and stillness, is what quiets the ego and its concern for the separate self that the world has taught us to be in the world. It is what gives us access to our deeper life in God. Poverty is the ultimate ground upon which our identity in God and God in us rests, but that requires a spiritual journey which ultimately leads to the death of the ego we created for the world, so as to be superior to the rest of God's children.

The reason the separate, independent self that we create to be in the world, and to be in the world in a better state than others, must die if we are to realize the fullness of the deeper life to which Jesus calls us is because Jesus' words make no sense to that self that we have created to be in the world.

Consider what Jesus says in Matthew's Gospel when asked which commandment is the greatest:

> "You shall love the Lord your God with all your heart, and with all your soul, and with all your mind." This is the greatest and first commandment. And the second is like it: "You shall love your neighbor as yourself." On these two commandments hang all the law and the prophets.[3]

If taken seriously, Jesus' words are impossible from the level of consciousness that we develop from being in the world. But what Jesus reveals to his disciples is a deeper level of consciousness from which we can experience loving God with all our heart, soul, and mind, and our neighbor as ourselves. We can experience that because we are no longer distracted by the illusion of the false self that we have created to be in the world so as to be better than all the other false selves in the world. This is our deepest level of consciousness and represents who we were in God and who God was in us before the world began making us into its likeness. Practicing this deepest level of consciousness is what prayer, at its deepest level, is all about.

From the level of consciousness that connects us to the world, it is impossible to love God with all our heart, soul, and mind, since the world demands that we give our attention to the needs of the flesh if we are to survive and prosper. Likewise, from the level of consciousness that connects us to the world, it is impossible to love our neighbor as ourselves, since from the perspective the world has given us, we are separate entities distinct from other human beings. In the world, we certainly *are* separate entities, but Jesus tells his followers that there is a deeper life and a deeper level of consciousness than that level of consciousness that connects us to the world.

This deeper level of consciousness is what Christian mystics and saints have been practicing for the last two thousand years. Prayer, at its deepest level, is the practice of this deeper level of consciousness, where we are no longer separate entities in the world, but have returned to who we were in God and who God was in us before the world began making us into its likeness.

The way we enter and come to practice this deeper level of consciousness is through the prayer of silence. Silence is not easily achieved, since the world presents us with an endless flow of one idea, thought, or feeling after another. Prayer, in its ultimate form, is all about getting to the silence and stillness of who we were in God and who God was in us before the world insisted that we create an ego (or separate self) that was different from others by being better or worse in terms of wealth, power, prestige, talent, beauty, or righteousness. Getting to this deepest core of our being and learning to live out of that unitive consciousness that we share with God and other human beings is the ultimate purpose of contemplative prayer.

It is not the purpose of this book to explain the contemplative practice of prayer, however. There are others far more competent at that. Thomas Keating, Richard Rohr, and Eckhart Tolle are excellent teachers of contemplative practice, and I highly recommend them. But let us remember that the ultimate purpose of contemplative prayer is not to get us to a more superior place in God than our neighbors, but to get us to a lesser place in the world, so we might see the beauty of Jesus' words and allow those living words to take root within us—to ultimately bring Jesus' kingdom to earth.

Jesus' words are the most beautiful words ever spoken, but their beauty cannot be seen from the level of consciousness that connects us to the world. Indeed, Jesus' words, from the level of consciousness that connects us to the world, make no sense. How can we possibly love our neighbor in the same way we love ourselves? From the perspective of the ego that we have created to be in the world, our neighbor is a different entity than ourselves and it is impossible to love them in the same way we love ourselves. But there is a deeper life and a deeper level of consciousness than the one we have developed by being in the world, and from this deeper level of consciousness it is possible to love God with all our heart, soul, and mind—and our neighbor as ourselves.[4] The spiritual journey into this deeper life to which Jesus calls us is one of transformation from the life we have created to be in the world to that deeper life of who we were in God and who God was in us before the world began molding us into its likeness.

From the level of consciousness that we have acquired by being in the world, our mind is a constant flow of one idea, thought, or emotion after another. The prayer of silence is the way we escape for a time the absolute hold that the world has upon us, and if we practice this prayer of silence enough, we can eventually get to a place from which we can see the beauty of Jesus' words. We can experience loving God with all of our heart, soul, and mind, and our neighbor as ourselves, because we are no longer limited to the perspective that the ego provides.

This is not where we begin the spiritual journey. We begin the spiritual journey from the perspective of the false self that we have created to be in the world, and from that perspective we see ourselves as either more than others or less than others. The world tells us to strive to be more than our neighbors and our enemies, but Jesus' teachings can only be ultimately realized by becoming less than others. The way we ultimately become less than others is by allowing the false self or ego to die so we might come to live out of who we are in God and who God is in us, rather than succumbing to the needs of the false self.

This is the dying that Jesus' disciples and the great saints and mystics throughout Christian history have experienced. But those people represent the end of the spiritual journey, not its beginnings. We nearly all begin the spiritual journey with little more than beliefs that purport to make us better in God's sight than other people, because when we begin the spiritual journey, we are almost always experiencing God through all the filters that we have created by being in the world. From that level of consciousness, the most beautiful words of Jesus make no sense. But there is a deeper level of consciousness from which we can experience the beauty of those words and want those living words to come to life within us.

This idea of unitive consciousness—being in another and another being in us—is certainly strange from the perspective the world has given us, and that is why it usually takes a lifetime of dying to the desires of the false self. The way this dying takes place is by paying attention to Jesus' words and seeing how impossible those words are from the level of consciousness that connects us to the world. Loving our neighbor, and even our enemy,[5] in the same way we love ourselves is not possible from the perspective of the egoic consciousness that connects us to the world. Thus, in the early stages of the spiritual journey, we tend to ignore the words of Jesus that address our deeper life in God, and instead trust our beliefs and those portions of the Bible that address our life in the world.

The reason this deeper life in God and God in us is necessary is because it is only from the perspective of our deeper life in God that we can see the beauty of Jesus' words, which are not telling us how to be righteous in the world, but how to bring Jesus' kingdom to earth. This is the ultimate purpose of the gospel, but early in the spiritual journey, where we are still operating out of the ego and our relationship with God centers on our ego needs, we have little understanding or interest in bringing Jesus' kingdom to earth.

From the egoic level of consciousness the most we can do with Jesus' words is to repent over them because we can see how impossible they are from our perspective in the world. But that is enough to get the spiritual journey started, since our repentance over Jesus' words is always followed by the overwhelming experience of God's mercy and forgiveness. Our transformation into Jesus' merciful and forgiving likeness only begins when we start to pay attention to Jesus' words, which are always telling us that our sin is deeper than we imagine.

Of course, since the spiritual journey usually doesn't begin with much more than a belief that purports to make us righteous, we can get stuck in that place of trusting our beliefs and avoiding the spiritual journey to which Jesus calls us for years. At the start of the spiritual journey, we usually have faith in our beliefs rather than in the words of Jesus. The ego loves our beliefs because they make the ego superior to other egos. The words of Jesus, however, are always pointing out our sin on ever deeper levels, so that we might experience mercy and forgiveness on ever deeper levels. This is the deeper life to which Jesus calls us, but the ego is usually quite content with its beliefs and wants to appear superior to other egos. The spiritual journey into the deeper life to which Jesus calls his followers, however, always centers on the words of Jesus. They reveal our sin at ever deeper levels, so that we might experience God's mercy and forgiveness at ever deeper levels..

Jesus is always calling us to a life deeper than the life of the ego, but this deeper life must be practiced! We must disassociate from the egoic level of consciousness that presents us with endless data connecting us to our concerns in the world. This is prayer at its deepest level, which alone allows us to really see the beauty of Jesus' words, but which make no sense to the ego. Jesus tells us to "give to everyone who begs from you, and do not refuse anyone who wants to borrow from you."[6] Of course, the ego will never go for this. We need to see if our giving will be appreciated and helpful. Someone once told me not to give money to homeless people because they just spend it on drugs. But our giving is not ultimately intended to aid others, but to free us from the egoic level of consciousness by giving away what the world values.

I was in a store at Christmas time, and a man in front of me was trying to pay for his groceries with gift cards that the cashier insisted had no money on them. The man was confused and didn't have any other way of paying for his things. The cashier called for the manager who was busy with another problem, so partially out of impatience because I was stuck online, and partially because it was Christmas, I told the cashier to put the forty-five dollars charge on my credit card. Both the cashier and another customer said how nice I was, but it did not produce a good feeling in me. If this was ten years earlier, this experience would have made me feel good about myself, but I am further along than I was ten years ago, and the experience brought me to repentance. It was such a rare experience, but it should have been the life out of which I am constantly living, rather than the rare exception—repentance should be my response to this good event, since only repentance brings us to the transformative experience of God's mercy and forgiveness. Feeling righteous only reinforces the ego and diverts us from the spiritual journey.

Giving ourselves away to the world, just like Jesus did, is the ultimate end of the spiritual journey, but it will require the death of the self-interested ego, that self that we and the world create. As we have said, Jesus was not more than other men, but less. By the time Jesus had reached the age of thirty, whatever ego had developed through his childhood, adolescence, and early adulthood had died, and Jesus had learned to operate exclusively out of that deeper level of consciousness of who he was in God and who God was in him. This is also the level of consciousness that the great Christian mystics and saints pursued, and it is open to all of us who are willing to allow the egoic self to die so that our deeper life in God might come forth.

False prophets and teachers are created when individuals claim to speak for God before the death of the false self. Claiming unitive consciousness from the perspective of the ego makes us appear to be more than our neighbors and our enemies, but Jesus' words are always calling us to be less and not more than who we were in God and who God was in us before the world began making us into its' likeness.

> Not everyone who says to me, "Lord, Lord," will enter the kingdom of heaven, but only the one who does the will of my Father in heaven. On that day many will say to me, "Lord, Lord, did we not prophesy in your name, and cast out demons in your name, and do many deeds of power in your name?" Then I will declare to them. "I never knew you; go away from me, you evildoers."[7]

The gospel is not about aggrandizing the false self that we have created to be in the world but about becoming those empty vessels through whom God's love, mercy, and forgiveness might flow to the world just as they had with Jesus. For that to happen, the egoic self that we have created to be in the world must die. This death process usually takes a lifetime, and throughout the early stages of the journey we are largely unaware of any deeper life than the one we have created to be in the world. From that level of consciousness, we can hold beliefs about Jesus paying for our sins, and we can act lovingly toward others, but if we still identify with the ego and its desire to be more than other people, we are still trapped in the false self that we have created to be in the world, and are not operating out of that deeper life that is intended to bring Jesus' kingdom to earth.

There is a deeper life and a deeper level of consciousness than the one we have developed by being in the world, and it is only from this deeper level of consciousness that we can see the beauty and goodness of Jesus' words. This deeper level of unitive consciousness which Jesus promises his disciples at the end of John's Gospel usually takes years to develop, since it is not a matter of acquiring something new but allowing something old to die. This is the journey that Christian mystics have been following for two thousand years.

Of course, it should be noted that early in the spiritual journey there may be attempts at the deeper life of the mystic, but before the false self has even begun the death process, such efforts will have the effect of inflating the ego and making oneself appear to be more than other followers of Jesus rather than less. In the early stages of the spiritual journey, attempts at mysticism—developing deeper levels of consciousness connecting us to God rather than the world—will inflate the ego and propagate the lie that we are more than other children of God rather than less. One of the hardest things to get about the gospel is that Jesus is not more than other human beings, but less—devoid of ego, just like his Father.

As we have said, by the age of thirty, Jesus had completed the spiritual journey and whatever false self that had been created throughout life had died. He had become that perfect, empty vessel through whom his Father's mercy, forgiveness, and love might flow to the world. Unlike Jesus, our attempts at the deeper life of the mystic are almost always initially attempts of the false self or ego. The mysticism of the false self may seek to prophesy and cast out demons, but these are early stages of the spiritual journey where the ego is still trying to assert itself as more rather than less than other human beings. The deeper mysticism of unitive consciousness only occurs through the progressive death of the false self, and through our transformation into that deeper life in God and God in us. This ultimate stage of the spiritual journey is not an enrichment of the self that we have created to be more than other human beings, but the ultimate poverty of the self: existence without ego. The ego is about enrichment and making ourselves appear to be more than other human beings, but the ultimate life to which Jesus calls his followers is one of becoming less rather than more until there is nothing left of us but who we were in God and who God was in us before the world began making us into its likeness.

So without ego, who are we? This deeper life in God and God in us is who God created before the world began making us into its likeness rather than the likeness of our Father God. Getting back to that deeper angelic state is what the spiritual journey is all about. The reason this deeper life and deeper level of consciousness is necessary is because from the level of consciousness that connects us to the world, the words of Jesus make no sense. Unlike the world and the ego it fashions into an identity within us that strives to have more than our neighbors —more wealth, power, prestige, beauty, strength, talent, or righteousness—Jesus calls his followers to that ultimate poverty of who they we were in God and who God was in them, before the world demanded that they create an ego, an ego constantly trying to prove itself better than other egos to reap the bounty that the world offers. By contrast, Jesus tells us that our greatest blessing is poverty or emptiness. "Blessed are the poor in spirit, for theirs is the kingdom of heaven."[8] The ego self that we have created to be in the world cannot see poverty as a blessing, but there is a deeper life than the one we have created to be in the world. Christian mystics have always known that a poverty of spirit or absence of ego is always the end toward which the spiritual journey proceeds. Most monastic orders, especially the contemplative orders, always set poverty as the foremost of their orders' vows. Poverty is our return to the angelic state of being in God and God being in us. This is the reduced state that Jesus revealed throughout his public ministry, and to which he calls his followers. This is what the great Christian mystics and saints have always known, but it seems to have culminated with the great Spanish mystics of the sixteenth century.

The next two centuries, dubbed the Age of Reason and the Enlightenment, turned our attention toward truth as something to know rather than a deeper way to be, and many of the Protestant denominations that appeared at the time stressed the importance of what we believed to be true rather the deeper way of being in God and God being in us.

The ultimate truth of the gospel, however, is not something to know and believe, but something to become. It involves the ontological truth of our being rather than an epistemological truth of what we claim to know and believe. Of course, it is not that what we believe has no place in the spiritual journey, but it is an early place in the journey, and if we get stuck there it can be a terminal place in the journey. The end of the spiritual journey is Jesus' living words coming to life within us, but those divine words cannot take root in the egoic self that we have created to be in the world.

Jesus' words are intended to bring his kingdom to earth, but they cannot take root in the person that we have created to be in the world. From the perspective that we have acquired from being in the world, we can start the spiritual journey with beliefs about the Nicene Creed or the Salvation Gospel, but the deeper life to which Jesus calls us is always about Jesus' words coming to life within us, and that is not possible from the perspective that we have created to be in the world.

Jesus' words to his disciples can only take root in that deeper life of who we were in God and who God was in us before the world began making us into its likeness. Again, if we attempt unitive consciousness before the ego has at least begun the process of dying, the idea of being in God and God being in us will merely inflate the ego and cause us to see ourselves as more than other human beings rather than less. The end of the spiritual journey is ultimately to become those empty vessels through whom Jesus' living words might come to life. But, as we have repeatedly said, Jesus' words cannot come to life in the ego that we and the world have created to be in the world, and to be in a better state in the world than others. That was the righteousness of the religious leaders of Jesus' day, which Jesus' teachings are always transcending. Sacred beliefs and righteous behavior are things the ego can do, but the ego cannot love its neighbor, and even its enemy, in the same way it loves itself, unless that self is who we were in God and who God was in us before the world caused us to develop an ego.

From the perspective of the ego, we cannot see the beauty of Jesus' words, so we try to find ways around them. Sacred beliefs are popular because they require little infringement upon the ego and can even add to the quest of the ego to be better than our neighbors and our enemies. Unfortunately, many people never venture beyond their sacred beliefs. Eternal life, however, is not on a pass/fail basis, but is determined by how much or how little of Jesus' words have come to life within us.

The Apostle Paul speaks of someone "caught up to the third heaven."[9] There are multiple levels of eternal life based upon how seriously we take the words of Jesus. Of course, the popular view from the perspective of the ego is that eternal life is on a pass/fail basis determined by our beliefs rather than the words of Jesus. This is the popular view because it offers the ultimate reward of heaven at the meager price of trusting our beliefs to save us rather than Jesus' words.

> I do not judge anyone who hears my words and does not keep them, for I came not to judge the world, but to save the world. The one who rejects me and does not receive my word has a judge; on the last day the words I have spoken will serve as judge.[10]

God does not judge us but allows us to judge ourselves by

the things we choose to love. Jesus tells us the best things to love and the worst things to love. How far we go in loving the things that Jesus tells us to love and avoiding the things that Jesus tells us not to love is what shapes where we begin eternal life. This is what makes Jesus' words so important and like no other words in the Bible.

Jesus' words are meant to reveal our sin at ever deeper levels so we might experience God's mercy and forgiveness at ever deeper levels. The spiritual journey is not one of becoming sinless but about becoming ever more merciful, forgiving, and loving for having received so much mercy, forgiveness, and love ourselves—because we have paid attention to Jesus' words and practiced the repentance to which his words constantly call us.

---

1. Matthew 6:14–15.
2. Matthew 7:22–23.
3. Matthew 22:37–40.
4. Ibid.
5. Matthew 5:44–45.
6. Matthew 5:42.
7. Matthew 7:21–23.
8. Matthew 5:3.
9. Second Corinthians 12:2.
10. John 12:47-48.

CHAPTER 6

OUR TRANSFORMATION INTO THE DEEPER LIFE TO WHICH JESUS CALLS US

This transformative journey into the deeper life to which Jesus calls us is essentially a spiritual journey through which the ego or false self, which we have created to be in the world, begins to die so our deeper life in God may come forth. The nature and character of our eternal being is shaped by how much of the ego, with its desire to be more than other people, is allowed to die so we might become those empty, angelic vessels through whom God's love, mercy, and forgiveness might pass to the world, just as they had through Jesus. Before the ego begins to die, we can act like we love others in the same way we love ourselves, but that is usually an act meant to embellish the image we wish to portray to others, rather than a love that springs spontaneously from our deeper life in God.

Of course, if we are still trusting our beliefs, righteous behavior, and our egos' interpretations of our spiritual experiences, we are still in the early stages of the spiritual journey. There is nothing wrong with that unless we get stuck there, which can easily happen, since, in the early stages of the spiritual journey, we are largely unaware of any deeper life. Sure, we may get glimpses from time to time, but the spiritual journey is about bringing that deeper life in God and God in us to the surface. It is about living out of that deeper life rather than living out of the egoic, false self that we have created to be in the world.

Unlike Jesus, however, who had completed the spiritual journey before the age of thirty and lived the three years of his public ministry out of that deeper life without an ego, most of us are somewhere amidst the journey that is the dying of the ego, allowing our deeper life in God and God in us to come forth. Seeing ourselves as better than our neighbors and our enemies is our deepest sin and what keeps us from the fullness of life to which Jesus calls us. Seeing ourselves as less than others because we are becoming those empty vessels devoid of ego is the ultimate end of the spiritual journey.

In the early stages of the spiritual journey, where we still operate out of the egoic level of consciousness, the awareness of our deeper life in God and God in us tends to inflate the ego and make us appear to be more than others in our relationship to God. But by the end of the spiritual journey, we become less than others, without an ego, so God's love, mercy, and forgiveness might freely flow through us to the world without interference from the ego, just as it had with Jesus.

Becoming less is the way to the deeper life, while becoming more is the way of the ego and the world. The path to the deeper life to which Jesus calls us is one of repentance over Jesus' words to his disciples.

> For if you forgive others their trespasses, your heavenly Father will also forgive you; but if you do not forgive others, neither will your Father forgive your trespasses.[1]

God allows us to judge ourselves by the way we judge others. Relating to others the way we want God to relate to us is a big part of the deeper life to which Jesus calls us. Of course, if we are still at the early stages of the spiritual journey and trusting our beliefs and righteousness to make us better than other people, we will always look to find detours around the hard words of Jesus, which are always calling us to a deeper life than the life we have created to be in the world. When we realize that God allows us to judge ourselves by the way we judge others, we have arrived at a latter stage of the spiritual journey, bringing us into a deeper intimacy with God. This deeper intimacy with God, where we treat others the way we want God to treat us, cannot be accomplished by the ego, whose desire is to be more than others. The idea that God will be toward us the way we are toward others is a big part of the deeper life to which Jesus is calling us. This is certainly unsettling to the ego, since the ego always wants to be judged by what makes it more than other people, like our beliefs and righteousness. Jesus, however, tells us that we will receive mercy and forgiveness in proportion to how much mercy and forgiveness we extend to others. This is the deeper life to which Jesus is always calling us, but to begin to experience this deeper life we need to spend time alone with God and Jesus' words. If we do, "...the Advocate, the Holy Spirit, whom the Father will send in my name, will teach you everything, and remind you of all that I have said to you." Being reminded of all that Jesus said should keep us in a blessed place of repentance for the rest of our lives. This is the deeper life that causes God's mercy and forgiveness to flow through us to the world, but getting there requires the death of the ego that we and the world have created to be in the world, and to be better off than other human beings. As we have said, we do not come to God by doing it right but by seeing how wrong we do it.

Of course, religion in most of its popular forms is largely about the early stages of the spiritual journey where we are living almost exclusively out of the egoic, false self that we have created to be in the world. Popular churches appeal to the ego and offer eternal life in exchange for beliefs and righteousness that make them better than their neighbors and their enemies.

This is not to reject the Salvation Gospel. It is the place from which many of us begin the spiritual journey, but it is not a good place to get stuck because it strengthens our attachment to the ego. Of course, many do get stuck there for years before the circumstances of their lives cause them to seek the deeper life to which Jesus calls us. It is easy to get stuck in our beliefs and righteousness, since so much of the Bible is about righteousness as the way we should be in the world, but Jesus is not telling us how to be righteous in the world. Jesus is telling us of a way to be that will bring his kingdom to earth. We are an evolving species, with Jesus as both the alpha and the omega of human history. He is the reason everything came into being and the end towards which all human history ultimately moves.

To realize that ultimate end of bringing Jesus' kingdom to earth in ourselves, we must get serious about Jesus' words, which are nothing like the rest of the Bible, but are living words meant to take root at the deepest core of our being so we can produce the heavenly fruit of his kingdom. This is certainly not the popular gospel, since it ultimately requires the death of the ego, which many of us are not willing to give up until our deathbeds, where our pretenses to be more than other human beings are no longer feasible. This dying process can be painful, but pain on one level of consciousness is what can cause us to seek a deeper level of consciousness, where pain is at least more tolerable. This is not an easy place to get to and must be practiced for years before the ego—which after all, is our connection to the world!—begins to lose its grip on us.

The ego wants what makes it better than other people; also, we believe that being free from pain goes a long way to making us feel better than other people. But suffering and pain can often aid in getting us to that deeper level of consciousness where we are in God and God is in us. This deeper unitive level of consciousness does not come about by simply praying and requesting it, although prayer at its deeper level is the path to the deeper life. Often people who experience life-changing events that prevent them from being better than other people find themselves discovering life on a deeper level. Jesus is always looking for people who have the potential to seek life on a deeper level because they see themselves as unable to be better than other people, because of handicaps, illness, or aging. The death of the ego may take many forms, but its demise is essential for our deeper life in God to come forth. So long as the ego is alive and well it is our highest and often our only priority, making it impossible to love God with all our heart, soul, and mind, and our neighbor as ourselves.[2] Loving God with all our heart, soul, and mind, and our neighbor as ourselves requires the angelic state of consciousness that we knew before we came into the world and began to develop an ego. The way we get back to that angelic state is by repenting over the words of Jesus. The consequent experience of God's mercy, forgiveness, and love will always be deeper still.

The problem with the initial stages of the spiritual journey is that our beliefs and righteous behavior can leave us in a state of righteousness where we can all too easily believe that we are ready for heaven just as we are. All we need do to stay in that blissful state is to avoid the words of Jesus, because those words constantly tell us that our sin is much deeper than we can imagine from the perspective the world has given us. What makes the words of Jesus so radically different from the rest of the Bible is that they are not telling us how to be righteous in the world, but how to bring Jesus' kingdom to earth. That requires much more than righteousness. It requires that we see our sin at ever deeper levels so we might experience God's mercy and forgiveness on ever deeper levels. Jesus tells his disciples, "Whoever comes to me and does not hate father and mother, brothers and sisters, yes, even life itself, cannot be my disciple."[3] Why would Jesus say something like that? In other places in the Bible, we are told to love our fathers and mothers, because much of the Bible is telling us how to be righteous in the world, which represents the early stages of the spiritual journey. But Jesus is telling his disciples how they must be if they are to bring his kingdom to earth. That requires a radically different way to be than how the world has taught us to be.

> While he was still speaking to the crowd, his mother and his brothers were standing outside, wanting to speak to him. Someone told him, "Look, your mother and brothers are standing outside, wanting to speak to you." But to the one who told him this, Jesus replied, "Who is my mother and who are my brothers?" And pointing to his disciples, he said, "Here are my mother and my brothers! For whoever does the will of my Father in heaven is my brother and sister and mother."[4]

The reason we love our particular fathers and mothers and our brothers and sisters is because they are ours and connected to us through our egos which see those things that are ours as special and better than the rest of the world. From the perspective of the ego, however, we cannot see that as evil. It is only from that deeper perspective of who we are in God and who God is in us that we can see the evil of the ego and its self-concern. From the perspective of the ego, righteousness is as far as we can go in the spiritual journey, because the deeper life to which Jesus calls his followers requires the death of the ego, so we can love our neighbors, and even our enemies, in the same way we love ourselves.

The unitive consciousness that Jesus describes to his disciples at the end of John's Gospel requires the death of the ego. Our life in the world is directed by ego and what will make us more than other human beings, but the life that Jesus calls us to is our life in God and God in us. There is no room for ego in the deeper life to which Jesus calls us. The fullness of life in God only comes about through the demise of the ego. For most of us, that does not happen in a moment of transformation into Jesus' likeness, although that is what the ego in us desires. For most of us, however, the ego dies slowly as its sins are exposed by the words of Jesus. If we pay attention to Jesus' words, we begin to see our need for mercy and forgiveness at ever deeper levels because we see our sin at ever deeper levels.

> "For I tell you, unless your righteousness exceeds that of the Pharisees you will never enter the kingdom of heaven."[5]

The righteousness that exceeds that of the Pharisees is the righteousness of mercy and forgiveness, which can only be experienced by seeing our sin at ever deeper levels because we pay attention the words of Jesus. We might like to imagine that our only problem is that we have sinned and need to be forgiven. Indeed, that is where many if not most spiritual journeys begin, but the end of the spiritual journey is to become those empty vessels through whom God's mercy, forgiveness, and love might pass to the world. Desiring to be forgiven is something the false self can do, but becoming forgiving and merciful is not something the false self can do. That requires the deeper life of who we are in God and who God is in us, which at the outset of the spiritual journey is almost unimaginable. However, it grows in proportion to how much ego death we are willing to suffer. We may begin the spiritual journey by seeking to be forgiven, but the purpose of Jesus' words, and the Holy Spirit who explains those words to us, is to become forgiving.

> For if you forgive others their trespasses, your heavenly Father will also forgive you; but if you do not forgive others, neither will your Father forgive your trespasses.[6]

God does not judge us at all because God is forgiving, but God does allow us to judge ourselves by the way we judge others.

> Do not judge, so that you may not be judged. For with the judgment you make you will be judged, and the measure you give will be the measure you get. Why do you see the speck in your neighbor's eye, but do not notice the log in your own eye?[7]

In answer to Jesus' question of why we see faults in others that we do not see in ourselves, the answer is that we live most of our life out of the false self or ego, rather than our deeper life in God, and it is only from our deeper life in God that we can see the false self for what it is. The egoic self is the self that the world creates through rewarding good behavior and punishing bad behavior. What the world deems as good behavior is behavior that distinguishes us as better than others. It begins with better grades in school, winning in athletic competitions, and acquiring more money, fame, or power than the competition. From this competitive perspective that the world has given us, we can read and love the Bible, but the hard words of Jesus to his disciples must be ignored, because they always speak of a deeper life than the life of the ego. The spiritual journey to which Jesus calls us, however, is always about trying to reduce us to love for others rather than love of self.

As we have seen, love exists in two distinct forms: the love of the world and the love of God. The love of the world is the love for those things that will make us appear to be better than other human beings in terms of wealth, power, prestige, beauty, strength, or piety. God, however, is in competition with no one, nor does God desire things that are lacking in the Divine. God's love is not a desire to acquire what God lacks, but a desire to create the nature of the Divine in his creation. The way this happens is through the spiritual journey to which Jesus has been calling his followers for the last two thousand years.

Of course, early in the spiritual journey we are still living out of the egoic, false self that we have created to be in the world. Jesus' words are meant to show the folly of such a life and point to our deeper life of being in God and God being in us. As we have said, if we try to realize this deeper level of unitive consciousness too early in the spiritual journey, where our egoic consciousness is still our dominant level of consciousness, it will inflate the ego and add to the illusion of the false self and its desire to be more than other human beings rather than less.

The nature of the spiritual journey is about getting back to who we were in God and who God was in us before the world began making us into its likeness, but if that happens too soon before the egoic, false self has sufficiently died, much of our spiritual experiences will tend to inflate the ego and cause us to see ourselves as more than others rather than less. Of course, this will never be the popular gospel, since most people throughout most of their lives are content with the righteousness that can be achieved by the ego, with its beliefs and righteous behavior, and might only begin to consider the death of the ego with the approach of old age and physical death.

We all do have eternal life, but the nature and character of that eternal life is not established by our beliefs and righteous behavior, but by how much or how little of Jesus' words have taken root within us. As we have seen, Jesus' words are the seeds of eternal life in its most heavenly form, but those living words can only take root in that heavenly soil of who we were in God and who God was in us before the world took hold of us and began making us into its likeness. The nature of Jesus' words to his disciples cannot take root in the egoic, false self that we have created to be in the world. In fact, we cannot even see the beauty of Jesus' words from the egoic level of consciousness that connects us to the world. From that perspective, there is nothing beautiful about loving even your enemies[8] and giving to all who beg from you.[9] But there is the deeper life to which Jesus calls his followers, and it is only from the perspective of this deeper life that we can see how beautiful it is to give ourselves away to others. Getting to this deeper life of giving ourselves away to God's creation just as God does is what the spiritual journey is all about.

The gospel is all about love, but love comes in two distinct forms: there is the love for God and his creation, and the love for those things that we imagine will make us appear to be more than other human beings. In the Gospels, Jesus tells us the best things to love and the worst things to love. Among the worst things to love, the love of money or wealth is very high on the list. Jesus' teachings against wealth or money appear in twelve different places throughout the Gospels.[10] What is so evil about money is that it is our major source of feeding the ego and its sense of superiority over other people, while Jesus is always calling us to be less than other people rather than more.

The thing that Jesus tells us we should love rather than money is poverty: being reduced to a love for God and his creation, rather than a love of self and all the pretenses we create to make ourselves appear to be more than our neighbors and our enemies. This is the ultimate end of the spiritual journey to which Jesus calls his followers. It is all about what we should love and what we should not love, because our eternal nature is being formed by the things we love. Heaven is not attained on a pass/fail basis depending upon what we have believed to be true about God and ourselves at a particular point in human history. The nature and character of our eternal being is determined by how much or how little of Jesus' living words have taken root at the deepest core of our being. That requires an enormous transformation from the person we are in the world to the person we are in God and how much God is in us. From the perspective that the world has given us, it is impossible to love God with all our heart, soul, and mind, and our neighbor as ourselves.[11] That is why the spiritual journey into our deeper life in God ultimately requires the death of the false self and its desire to be thought of as more than our neighbors and our enemies. Getting to the emptiness of who we are in God and who God is in us is what creates a place where Jesus' words might take root within us.

The first stage of the spiritual journey is about getting us beyond our beliefs, beyond the idea that those beliefs make us better than other people. The first step in the spiritual journey may be getting beyond the idea that trusting in our beliefs will save us, but going beyond beliefs does not yet undermine the egoic level of consciousness by which the world has taught us to direct our lives. If the egoic level of consciousness remains our dominant level of consciousness, the next stage of the spiritual journey is one of righteousness. We see this level of consciousness throughout the Old Testament. It was represented in Jesus' time by most of the religious leaders of his day.

The righteous stage of the spiritual journey does take us beyond our beliefs, but it does little to get us beyond the egoic, false self that tells us how to be better than our neighbors and our enemies. Getting beyond this stage of righteousness in the spiritual journey ultimately requires the death of the ego which has created the false self. But the ego does not die easily or in one divine moment! In fact, the ego cannot die until there is a deeper life to replace it. What makes this deeper life so different from the ego is that it has no self-interest, but is directed by God's interest. This is the deeper life that Jesus reveals in the Gospels and calls his disciples to follow. It is not an ascent into a more heavenly state of egoic bliss, but a descent into our deeper life in God. As we have said, it is largely a long process of returning to the angelic state of wanting nothing but God's will to come forth in our lives, just as it had with Jesus. Before we came into the world, we were those angelic beings who were created to do God's will, and love as God loves by giving ourselves away to others just as God gives himself away to the world. This is the ultimate end of the spiritual journey, but it requires a lifetime of dying to the egoic self and its love for the things that make us appear to be more than our neighbors and our enemies.

Becoming less rather than more is the deeper life to which Jesus calls us. As we have said, Jesus had no ego, but had become, by the age of thirty, that empty vessel through whom God's mercy, forgiveness, and love might flow to the world. This is also the deeper life to which Jesus calls his followers as well. It is about refusing to see ourselves as more than others, but seeing ourselves in others and others in us. This unitive consciousness allows us a perspective from which we can love our neighbors and even our enemies in the same way we love ourselves. This is not something that can be done by the ego, and this is the reason that the spiritual journey always moves toward the death of the ego, so our deeper life in God and God in us might begin to appear.

Of course, an awareness of this deeper life in God and God in us can be delayed for years by what so often follows our beliefs: our righteous behavior. Righteousness is often the typical next stage that reinforces our beliefs and keeps us from the deeper life to which Jesus calls his followers. Righteousness has great appeal to the false self that we create to be in the world, because it, like our beliefs, makes us appear to be better in God's sight than others. Righteousness, like our beliefs, is not much different from things like wealth, power, and prestige in that it inflates the ego and makes it impossible to love others in the same way we love ourselves.

Jesus has numerous teachings against the righteousness that makes us appear to be better than other people. Three of these stories appear in Luke's Gospel. In the story of the good Samaritan,[12] Jesus compares the righteousness of a priest and a Levite, who are intent upon righteousness as the avoidance of sin, with the compassion of a Samaritan, who a priest and a Levite would have seen as a sinner because of his wrong beliefs. In Jesus' teachings, love of others always trumps and represents later stages of the spiritual journey than our righteous beliefs and behavior.

Likewise, in the Parable of Prodigal son,[13] we hear of a man who had two sons, one righteous and one a prodigal. The prodigal experiences mercy and forgiveness in a way that eludes the righteous brother. The older, righteous brother thinks that his righteousness should put him in better stead with his father, and he wants to be rewarded for his righteousness with preferential treatment from his father, rather than wanting to be like his father in terms of mercy and forgiveness toward his brother.

Many people believe that righteousness is the end of the spiritual journey; much of the Old Testament can be used to support that claim. But according to Jesus, righteousness is a very early stage in the spiritual journey. Here is the third story that Jesus uses to confirm this.

> Two men went up to the temple to pray, one a Pharisee and the other a tax collector. The Pharisee, standing by himself, was praying thus, "God, I thank you that I am not like other people: thieves, rogues, adulterers, or even like this tax collector. I fast twice a week; I give a tenth of all my income." But the tax collector, standing far off, would not even look up to heaven,

but was beating his breast and saying, "God be merciful to me, a sinner!" I tell you, this man went down to his home justified rather than the other; for all who exalt themselves will be humbled, but all who humble themselves will be exalted.[14]

Righteousness is where so many religious people get stuck in their spiritual journey. The reason righteousness is so popular and why we can easily get stuck there is because it is something the ego can be to appear better than homosexuals or abortionists. Jesus' remedy for righteousness is to reveal our sin at ever deeper levels so none can boast.

What all three of the parables above reveal is that mercy and forgiveness are greater than righteousness and represent a later stage in the spiritual journey of our descent into who we are in God and who God is in us. Jesus' teachings are always calling us to a deeper life of repentance. For we must repent of being the person the world has created to be better than other people, rather than who our Father God had created to bring his kingdom to earth.

Righteousness is a stage in the spiritual journey, but it is an early stage that appeals to the ego, while the ultimate end of the spiritual journey always involves the death of the ego, since the ego is not God's creation but the world's. The journey back to who we are in God ultimately requires the death of the ego. But that is usually a very long and painful process, if we enter the process at all.

Jesus instructs his followers to love God and other human beings so completely that there is no love left over for the self that we have created to be in the world, and to be in the world in a better state than our neighbors and our enemies.[15] This deeper life is the angelic state of who we were before the world began teaching us to love ourselves more than others. Getting back to who we were in God, and who God was in us before we began to develop an ego is ultimately what the Gospel is all about.

There is no ego or self-love in a Triune God, which constantly gives itself away to one another. The Divine needs nothing. Jesus tells his followers that they can be like the Divine if they abide in him and he abides in them.

What causes us to be apart from God is the ego, which we have developed to be in the world, and to be in the world in a better state than our neighbors and our enemies. How much ego death we are willing to suffer is what determines how far we go in the spiritual journey and where we begin eternal life. Becoming those empty vessels through whom God's mercy, forgiveness, and love might freely flow to the world is essentially a matter of no longer being governed by the ego, because we recognize that the blessed place to which Jesus calls us is a place of being less than others rather than being more, because our ego is in the middle of a death process. This is what it means to be reduced to love.

What is so interesting about the spiritual journey to which Jesus calls us is that after the initial phases of beliefs and righteous behavior, we do not proceed deeper into the journey by doing it right, but by seeing how wrong we do it. Repentance is the holiness of the deeper life, and we do not get to the deeper places of the spiritual journey by doing it right, but by paying attention to Jesus' words and seeing how wrong we do things. Our transformation into Jesus' merciful and forgiving likeness does not happen through our beliefs and righteous behavior, although they are usually the early stages into the deeper life to which Jesus calls us. That deeper life is always about Jesus' living words coming to life within us and thus bringing his kingdom to earth through us. As we have seen, however, Jesus' words cannot take root in the person we have created to be in the world, but only in our deeper life in God.

Righteousness does not get us very far on the path to this

deeper life to which Jesus calls his followers, as he was always pointing out to the righteous religious leaders of his day. We only begin to enter the deeper life through repentance over Jesus' words, which reveal the great depth of our sin, and lead us to understand that God's mercy and forgiveness always reach deeper still. The life to which Jesus calls his followers is a deeper life than a life of righteousness, which has much more appeal to the ego. Early in the journey we are operating almost exclusively out of ego, or the self that we have created to be in the world, and to be in the world in a state that strives to find some way to be better than others.

As we have said, however, getting to this deeper life in God and God in us is not something that the person that we have created to be in the world can do. Indeed, our deeper life in God only comes forth through the death of the ego. This is what Christian mystics and saints have always known but it is certainly not the popular view, since the life that we have created to be in the world does not die easily, and Jesus' words cannot take root within the person that we have created to be in the world. There is, however, that deeper life that God had created before the world began making us into its likeness. The way we get back to this deeper life is through repentance over Jesus' words.

> Therefore do not worry, saying, "What will we eat?" or "What will we drink?" or "What will we wear?" For it is the Gentiles who strive for all these things; and indeed your heavenly Father knows that you need all these things. But strive first for the kingdom of God and his righteousness, and all these things will be given to you as well.[16]

The deeper life to which Jesus calls his followers is not something that seems feasible from the perspective of the false self that we have created to be in the world. If we pay attention to Jesus' words and think about the strange things he says, we can see that the things he tells us to do are impossible from the level of consciousness that we have acquired by being in the world. From the level of consciousness that the world has given us, it is natural to pursue the ways of the world, to strive to be more than other individuals to assure our survival and well-being. But from the deeper life to which Jesus calls us, it becomes clear that the deeper life is not a matter of being more than our neighbors and our enemies, but about being less. It is about being no more than those empty vessels through whom God's mercy, forgiveness, and love might pass to the world, just as they had with Jesus.

Of course, few of us ever come close to the emptiness of self that Jesus had achieved in order that his Father's love, mercy, and forgiveness might pass through him to the world. But however far we do progress is what determines where we begin eternal life. As we have said, eternal life is not granted on a pass/fail basis! Where we begin eternal life is a matter of how much or how little of Jesus' words have taken root at the deepest core of our being.

We may begin the spiritual journey with beliefs that we believe make us better than other people in God's sight. But the end of the spiritual journey is always about being reduced to no more than love for God and his creation. What limits how far we go in the spiritual journey is determined by how much ego death we are willing to bear, so our deeper life in God and God in us might come forth.

---

1. Matthew 6:14–15.
2. Matthew 22:37–39.
3. Luke 14:26.
4. Matthew 12:46–50.
5. Matthew 5:20.
6. Matthew 6:14–15.
7. Matthew 7:1–2.

8. Matthew 5:44.
9. Matthew 5:42.
10. Luke 16:19–26. Matthew 6:19-21. Luke 6:24. Matthew 13:22; also see Mark 4:19, and Luke 8:14. Matthew 19:24; also see Mark 10:23–25 and Luke 18:24. Luke 12:16–21. And Matthew 6:24, also see Luke 16:13.
11. Matthew 22:37–40.
12. Luke 10:25–37.
13. Luke 15:11–32.
14. Luke 18:10–14.
15. Matthew 22:36–40.
16. Matthew 6:31–33.

CHAPTER 7
THE PRACTICE OF THE DEEPER LIFE AND THE WORDS OF JESUS

The practice of the deeper life is not a matter of doing it right, but rather about paying attention to Jesus' words and therein seeing how wrong we do it. This keeps us in an almost constant state of repentance and subsequently grants us the experience of God's mercy and forgiveness. This is the nature of the deeper life to which Jesus calls his followers, but it certainly isn't the popular view.

In the early stages of the spiritual journey, we can feel quite content trusting our beliefs and righteous behavior to assure us that we are special and better in God's sight than our neighbors and enemies. But to remain in that place, we must avoid the words of Jesus, which tell a very different story. Jesus doesn't call his followers to righteousness, but to repentance on ever deeper levels. Of course, most of us, especially early in the journey, are quite content with our beliefs and righteous behavior to put us in good stead with God. But to remain in that place, we must avoid the words of Jesus to his disciples, which constantly reveal our sin at ever deeper levels. The blessing that follows from seeing our sin at ever deeper levels is the experience of God's mercy and forgiveness at ever deeper levels. This is the path to the deeper life, but it has no appeal to the ego, which wants us to see ourselves as better than others through our beliefs and behavior.

This deeper life of paying attention to Jesus' words and living in an almost constant state of repentance over his words is a deeper place in the spiritual journey, but it requires the death of the ego. Jesus did not make himself better than other people, but less than other people, egoless, so his Father's love, mercy, and forgiveness might freely flow through him to the world. This is what Jesus is trying to teach his disciples as well.

The righteousness that we experience in the early stages of the spiritual journey does not bring Jesus' kingdom to earth, but it is does appeal to the ego. Popular churches appeal to our egos since that is where most people are throughout most of our lives. The deeper life to which Jesus calls us, however, requires the death of the ego and our descent into our deeper life in God.

> Whoever comes to me and does not hate father and mother, wife and children, brothers and sisters, yes, even life itself, cannot be my disciple.[1]

These words of Jesus to his followers speak of the deeper life to which Jesus calls us, but this deeper life requires a deeper identity in God that is enormously different from the identity we have created for ourselves to be in the world. Jesus goes on in this section of Luke's Gospel where he describes the cost of discipleship by saying, "So therefore, none of you can become my disciples if you do not give up all your possessions."[2] Our possessions are what connect us to the world through our egos, which make some people appear to be more than others. But the point of the gospel is to become less than others in order that God's mercy, forgiveness, and love might flow through us to the world, without being hampered by the self-interest of the ego. This is the end of the spiritual journey to which Jesus calls his followers. How close we come to this ultimate end is what determines the nature and character of our consciousness and identity as we begin eternal life.

The way we pursue this deeper life is through repentance at ever deeper levels because we pay attention to Jesus' words and see our sin at ever deeper levels. Many people never get to this point in the journey because they get stuck in the righteousness that their beliefs and righteous behavior provide. That is as much of the gospel as their life in the world can bear. But even so, there is a deeper life to which Jesus' words are always calling us.

Our lives are journeys through which God allows us to create the nature and character of our own eternal beings by the things we choose to love. This is the enormous freedom God has given human beings. How far we go into this deeper life to which Jesus calls us is determined by how much repentance—changing of our minds concerning who we are and what we love—we are willing to bear. Initially, the spiritual journey may only involve a change of beliefs and behavior, but if we continue to spend time alone with God and Jesus' words, we begin to see our sin at ever deeper levels. This deeper life to which Jesus calls us is not one of making ourselves more than other people, but less—just like Jesus.

Of course, few churches can preach this message without quickly going out of business, since this is the end of the spiritual journey, which most people will avoid until it becomes obvious that their life in the world is passing away. As we approach physical death, it becomes easier to realize the illusion that we have tried to create by being in the world in a better state than others, instead of in a lesser state. Poverty is our greatest virtue. But that is impossible to see from the egoic level of consciousness that connects us to the world.

Jesus' words, however, are always telling his followers of a deeper life than the one that the world has caused us to develop through acculturation. Getting back to this deeper life of who we were in God and who God was in us before the world began making us into its likeness is what the spiritual journey is all about. The reason we must get back to that deeper life is because the living words of Jesus, which are meant to take root within us and produce the fruit of his kingdom, cannot take root within the egoic, false self that we and the world have created. As we have previously said, this is why Jesus tells Nicodemus, "You must be born from above."[3] Being born from above is a matter of getting back to who we were in God and who God was in us before the world began making us into its likeness. Our rebirth into this deeper life to which Jesus calls us does not happen in a single historical moment the way our birth into the world happened, however, but through the progressive death of the life we have created to be in the world in order that our deeper life in God and God in us might come forth.

Of course, at the beginning of the spiritual journey we are hardly aware of any life besides that life that we have created for ourselves to be in the world. This is where most of us begin the spiritual journey, but it is also where so many get stuck. Early in the spiritual journey we have little or no understanding of the deeper life so we imagine that spiritual growth is a matter of receiving spiritual gifts that make some believers appear to be more than others, while the spiritual growth of which Jesus speaks is always a descent into who we were in God and who God was in us before the world began making us into its likeness.

> At that time the disciples came to Jesus and asked, "Who is greatest in the kingdom of heaven?" He called a child, whom he put among them, and said, "Truly I tell you, unless you change and become like children, you will never enter the

kingdom of heaven. Whoever becomes humble like this child is greatest in the kingdom of heaven..."[4]

This is the deeper, angelic life to which Jesus is always calling his disciples. But getting to this deeper life always involves the death of the ego, which we have created to be in the world in a better state than our neighbors and our enemies. How far we progress into this deeper life is largely determined by how much death to the ego we are willing to bear. As the ego begins to die, our deeper life in God and God in us begins to come forth. This is what the great saints and mystics have always known.

The ultimate truth of the gospel is pragmatic. It is not determined by what we believe to be true, but by how much of Jesus' living words have come to life within us. Jesus' words are heavenly words and as such they cannot take root within the person we have created to be in the world. In the world, we are told to love our fathers and mothers, wives and children, brothers and sisters, because they are what are unique to us, and if they are better than other fathers, mothers, wives, children, brothers, and sisters, *ipso facto,* we ourselves are better. We take pride in our families being better than other families and we take pride in loving them more than others. This is seen as a virtue from our perspective in the world. But from the perspective of our deeper life in God it is the sin that keeps us connected to the world rather than the heavenly kingdom to which Jesus calls us.

> As they were going along the road, someone said to him, "I will follow you wherever you go." And Jesus said to him, "Foxes have holes, and birds of the air have nests; but the Son of Man has nowhere to lay his head." To another he said, "Follow me." But he said, "Lord, first let me go and bury my father." But Jesus said to him, "Let the dead bury their own

dead; but as for you, go and proclaim the kingdom of God." Another said, "I will follow you, Lord; but let me first say farewell to those at my home." Jesus said to him, "No one who puts a hand to the plow and looks back is fit for the kingdom of God."[5]

The person that we and the world have created to be in the world is not fit for the kingdom. That is the point that Jesus is making here. Living a life of repentance for not living out of the deeper life to which Jesus calls us, however, is what causes us to become the recipients of God's transformative mercy and forgiveness. We all fall short of the deeper life to which Jesus calls us, but that is the very thing that keeps us in a state of repentance and generates the unending mercy and forgiveness that follows from our repentance. We do not get to the deeper life to which Jesus calls us by doing it right, but by seeing how wrong we do it. Doing it right and being better than others is what the ego strives for, but Jesus' words are always calling us to that deeper life of repentance and the experience of God's mercy and forgiveness, by seeing how wrong we do it.

Much of the Bible is telling us how to be righteous, which can be as appealing to the ego as things like wealth, power, and prestige, since it distinguishes us as more than other human beings. Jesus, however, is not telling us how to be righteous, but how to bring his kingdom to earth, and that requires a deeper life than the life we have created to be in the world.

That, however, is not the popular gospel with which we usually begin the spiritual journey. The popular gospel is one that offers a heavenly eternal life in exchange for the belief that Jesus' death on the cross was payment for our sins, and with our sins being paid for we are now righteous and ready for heaven. Again, this is not a false gospel, but rather this era's popular cultural belief that gets the spiritual journey started. Where else would we begin the spiritual journey but with the only life with which we are familiar? When Jesus speaks of the deeper life of our being in God and God being in us,[6] he is speaking to who we were in God and who God was in us before the world began making us into its likeness. This is the deeper life to which Jesus calls his followers, but it ultimately requires the death of the ego or the false self that we have created to be in the world. This death to which Jesus calls his followers is a slow death that can take a lifetime, and many ignore it until their actual deathbed.

Jesus' words make little sense from the perspective the world has given us, and for that reason we usually prefer other portions of scripture over his words. Much of the Bible is speaking to the person we have created to be in the world, but Jesus' words to his disciples are ultimately speaking to who they are in God and who God is in them. This is the deeper life that is the end of the spiritual journey. How close we come to that end is what determines where we begin eternal life. Getting back to our original angelic, unitive consciousness is only achieved through the death of the false self, which essentially dies through neglect as we give ourselves increasingly to our deeper life in God.

The way we ultimately bring Jesus' kingdom to earth is by repenting over Jesus' words, which gives the Father permission to prune those areas of our lives that are preventing the words of Jesus from taking root within us. Of course, these are the latter stages of the spiritual journey, and throughout most of our lives we much prefer those sections of the Bible that instruct us concerning how to be righteous in the world. However, Jesus' words to his disciples are instructions concerning how to bring Jesus' kingdom to earth. Historically, God meets us in the world and attempts to show us through the Bible how best to be in the world, but God's ultimate plan is to bring his kingdom to earth. Of course, that requires an enormous transformation—from the person we have created to be in the world to a follower of Jesus who is able to bring heaven to earth by being completely different than the way the world has taught us to be.

In the early stages of the spiritual journey our beliefs and righteous behavior can make us appear to be more than other people, but in the later stages of the journey we see that God is calling us to be less than others and to operate without an ego or false self just as Jesus had. This deeper life of living without an ego is impossible from the perspective the world has given us. The egoic, false self that we create to be in the world can both believe and act righteously, but Jesus' living words cannot come to life within that self. To love your neighbor in the same way you love yourself requires the deeper life to which Jesus calls his followers. Only who we are in God and who God is in us gets us to the place of unitive consciousness where we can see ourselves in our neighbors and even in our enemies, and where we can love them somehow in the same way we love ourselves. That requires a different level of consciousness and a different level of being.

Only who we are in God and who God is in us can get us to the place from which we can love God with all of our heart, soul, and mind, and our neighbor as ourselves[7]—with no love left over for the egoic, false self that tries to convince our neighbors, our enemies, and even God that we are better than other people. The end of the spiritual journey is to love the way that God loves, by giving ourselves away to God's creation the same way that God gives himself away to his creation.

Just as Jesus himself reached the end of the spiritual journey, no longer coveting those things the world tells us will make us appear to be more than other individuals, Jesus calls his followers to that same end. This is the work of a lifetime. Whenever our time alone with God brings us to think that we have achieved that unitive state, the Holy Spirit reminds us of the words of Jesus: "But the Advocate, the Holy Spirit, whom the Father will send in my name, will teach you everything, and remind you of all that I have said to you."[8] The hard words of Jesus constantly remind us that we are not yet at the end of the journey, that we are in need of more repentance over Jesus' words, so we can experience the flood of God's mercy and forgiveness that prepares a place for Jesus' words to take root in the deepest core of our being. God's mercy and forgiveness are what prepare a place for Jesus' words to take root within us, but only our repentance over Jesus' words initiates God's mercy and forgiveness.

If we spend time alone with God, the Holy Spirit reminds us of those words of Jesus that are appropriate to where we at in the spiritual journey. If we get stuck in the early places in the journey where we are still trusting our beliefs and righteous behavior, there is little that the Holy Spirit can reveal concerning the words of Jesus, since so much of what Jesus has to say to his disciples is about our deeper life in God and God in us. That deeper life is always calling us to be less than other people, or to restore us to that angelic state before we developed an ego by being in the world. This is the angelic state that can be experienced in prayer in its deepest contemplative states.

Unfortunately, in the early stages of the spiritual journey, our religious beliefs and righteous behavior have the opposite effect: they make us appear to be better than other people, just like wealth, power, and prestige. But on the contrary, the words of Jesus are constantly revealing our sin at ever deeper levels to keep us on a journey of repentance where we experience the constant flow of God's mercy, forgiveness, and love passing through us to the world.

The truth of the gospel may begin as an epistemological truth or something to know and believe, but the end of the gospel is an ontological truth or a way to be. It happens because Jesus' words have taken root at the deepest core of our being and are producing heavenly fruit. We proceed in this spiritual journey to which Jesus calls us through a process of transformation: from the person we have created to be in the world to the person God desires to create to bring his kingdom to earth. This transformation does not happen in a moment of inspiration, but through a lifetime of dying to the desires of the ego, allowing God's deeper purposes to come forth in our lives. How much ego death we are willing to bear goes a long way in establishing how much of Jesus' words can take root within us, since so much of Jesus' words make no sense from the perspective of the ego that we have created to be in the world.

The mind or level of consciousness that we have acquired through our acculturation into the world does everything out of self-interest. That is because from our level of consciousness in the world, we are conscious subjects surrounded by a world of objects, many of which are subjects themselves whose interests are very different than our own. This is the environment in which the egoic, false self develops through childhood, adolescence, and early adulthood. The ego exists in a transactional world where we compete with other egos for those scarce resources that will give us the appearance of being either better than other human beings or worse than other human beings. The words of Jesus are always calling his followers to see themselves as less than others so they might experience the fullness of God's mercy, forgiveness, and love passing through them to the world, just as it was with Jesus.

> This saying is sure and worthy of full acceptance, that Christ Jesus came into the world to save sinners—of whom I am foremost. But for that very reason I received mercy, so that in me, as the foremost, Jesus Christ might display the utmost patience, making me an example to those who would come to believe in him for eternal life.[9]

Righteousness is not the path to the deeper life to which Jesus calls us, but it is an early place in the journey, so long as we don't get stuck there. The deeper life to which Jesus calls us is ultimately about coming into the deeper unitive consciousness that Jesus promises toward the end of John's Gospel. Of course, this unitive consciousness that Jesus promises his followers can never be realized by the ego. Being in Jesus and Jesus being in us can only come about through the death of the ego, since any assertion by the ego that it is in Jesus and Jesus is in it will be no more than a pretense.

When we view the things that Jesus said and did from the perspective of the ego, we want to be like Jesus by being better than other people. But Jesus is better than others by being less than others—by being completely devoid of ego. Jesus desired to give himself away, just like his Father is constantly giving himself away to his creation.

Of course, this is not our initial concept of God. Initially, from the perspective we have acquired by being in the world, we conceive of God as the person we would be if we were the creator and maintainer of the universe. From the perspective of our egos, we would expect worship and obedience from our creation. But a triune God does not have an ego. Instead, it is constantly giving itself away to the other members of the Godhead in acts of love. God has no desire to acquire anything, since God lacks nothing. His only desire is to give mercy, forgiveness, and love away to those who would receive it and be transformed into God's own merciful, forgiving, and loving likeness by having received it. That, however, is not so easily accomplished, since being the instrument through whom God's love, mercy, and forgiveness is given to the world is not something the ego can realize. The ego wants God's love, mercy, and forgiveness, but it wants it for itself in order to be special— better, more important, richer, more talented, more desirable than other people—that is the nature of the world and the ego that our acculturation into the world creates. Righteousness is as far as the ego can go in the spiritual journey. There is a deeper place in the spiritual journey, but it ultimately requires the death of the ego.

As we have said, to follow Jesus and have his living words come to life within us requires a deeper life than the life of the ego. The ego cannot love our neighbor in the same way it loves itself. The ego lives in a dualistic world where we are the subject in a world of objects. The well-being of ourselves as a subject is dependent upon how well we negotiate our interaction with the objective world that surrounds us. At the end of John's Gospel, however, Jesus offers his followers an entirely different way to be.

> If you love me, you will keep my commandments. And I will ask the Father, and he will give you another Advocate, to be with you forever. This is the Spirit of truth, whom the world cannot receive, because it neither sees him nor knows him. You know him, because he abides with you, and he will be in you.[10]

The problem with the Spirit being in us is that if we try to make that happen too early in the spiritual journey, it will have the negative effect of inflating the ego. Early in the spiritual journey, when we are still operating largely out of egoic consciousness, our desire is to be like Jesus the miracle worker, who casts out demons, prophesies, and reveals a power that is greater than other human beings. The deeper life to which Jesus calls us, however, is a life of being less than other men, which ultimately requires the death of the ego so we might become those empty vessels through whom God's love, mercy, and forgiveness might pass to the world untainted by our egos.

Our beliefs and righteous behavior are done on behalf of the ego, but being God's instruments of love, mercy, and forgiveness to the world requires a deeper life—the deeper life of who we were in God and who God was in us before the world forced us through acculturation to develop an ego desiring to be better than the rest of God's creation. Unfortunately, this ego is the point from which we usually begin the transformative, spiritual journey into Jesus' likeness. This process may take many years or decades, because the false self is not keen on dying, but the more it dies, the more our deeper life in God and God in us begins to come forth.

Of course, many people are oblivious to the fact that they even have an ego. It is simply who they are. The only way we start to become aware of our ego is through the practice of prayer at the deepest level of our being. From the level of who we are in God and who God is in us, we can see the illusion of the egoic false self which the world insists that we create. The ego is created through our acculturation in the world, but there is also the deeper life of who we were in God and who God was in us before acculturation. This is the deeper life we are trying to get back to through the spiritual journey of transformation.

Essential to this transformational journey is the practice of the prayer of silence. Contemplative silence is a deeper level of consciousness than the level of consciousness that connects us to the world. Silence is what opens us to experience our deeper life in God and God in us. It is what connects our branch to the vine.[11] The practice of this deeper life is also what eventually produces the death of the ego, since it is only from the perspective of our deeper life in God that we can see the folly of the ego and its pretenses to wealth, power, prestige, beauty, strength, or righteousness.

God is full of love, mercy, and forgiveness that he wants to pass through us to the world, but if our egos represent the level of consciousness out of which we operate, we get to decide who gets God's love, mercy, and forgiveness, and who are not deserving. From our deeper level of consciousness of who we are in

God and who God is in us, however, we are unable to discriminate, since that is the job of the ego. From the egoic level of consciousness we decide who is deserving of God's love and who is not deserving based upon how closely others resemble our notions of righteousness, rather than Jesus' words to forgive everyone[12] and judge no one.[13]

Of course, people will be quick to site scriptures that encourage us to judge, and insist that forgiveness is not for everyone. But this belief represents the early stages of the spiritual journey where we are still entrenched in the world. When we begin to practice the deeper life of prayer, the world begins to lose its grip upon us. The way the world maintains its hold upon us is through that constant flow of one idea or piece of data after another, so fast and unrelenting that our minds have no choice but to address that constant flow that presents itself to our consciousness. The only way to stop this endless flow of ideas is the contemplative practice of silence. Christian mystics in the early centuries of Christianity began practicing contemplative silence to see the beauty of Jesus' words that cannot be seen from the level of consciousness that we have acquired by being in the world. Many of Jesus' words make little or no sense from the perspective the world has given us, but mystics have discovered a deeper level of consciousness from which we can experience the beauty of loving our neighbor, and even our enemy, in the same way we love ourselves. This deeper level of consciousness is our deeper life in God and God in us, but it must be practiced and practiced for years before it can replace the egoic level of consciousness out of which we have been taught by the world to operate.

This practice of the deeper life of contemplation began with the early desert fathers and mothers, but was later taken up in the monastic tradition and flourished throughout the Middle Ages, reaching perhaps its high point with the great Spanish mystics of the sixteenth century. Unfortunately, the seventeenth and eighteenth centuries would move the western world in a very different direction. The title given to the seventeenth century was The Age of Reason, and the eighteenth century was dubbed The Enlightenment. Throughout these two centuries our cultural interest in truth changed from the deeper way of being that the mystics pursued, to truth as something to know and know scientifically in the same way that we know mathematical truth as objective, certain, and precise.

This scientific revolution of the modern period had an enormous effect upon Christian history as well. The Christian mysticism which had flourished throughout the ancient and medieval period was not something to simply know and know in the same way we know mathematics. The mysticism of the ancient and medieval worlds was not about knowing, but about living—living a deeper life and experiencing a different way to be connected to God rather than the world.

The acculturation of the modern period had an enormous effect upon the protestant denominations that developed at that time, stressing the importance of beliefs—what people believed to be true concerning God and his relationship with human beings—rather than the deeper life. One's faith became more a matter of what one believed to be true about God, rather than the embodiment of Jesus' words, which call us to perceive our sin at ever deeper levels so we might experience God's forgiveness and mercy at ever deeper levels.

The modern move toward science and truth as something to know with certainty after the model of mathematics, however, did not completely eradicate human beings' thirst for a deeper life in God. Our time has seen a renewed interest in mysticism. Mysticism represents a later stage of the spiritual journey, since mysticism requires the progressive death of the ego in order that our deeper life in God may come forth. In the early stages of the spiritual journey our beliefs and righteous behavior are usually sufficient, so long as we avoid the hard words of Jesus, which are always calling us to a deeper life in God and God in us. This deeper unitive consciousness requires a long practice of prayer whereby we set time apart each day to practice, in silence, an awareness of God's presence in our life. Silence is what breaks the hold the world has upon the level of consciousness connecting us to the world. Of course, silence can also open us to experiences that are not necessarily Divine. My rule is that the only thing that I allow to interrupt the silence is the Holy Spirit's reminding us of all that Jesus has said. "But the Advocate, the Holy Spirit, whom the Father will send in my name, will teach you everything, and remind you of all that I have said to you."[14]

If we practice this deeper life and deeper level of consciousness enough that it becomes our preferred level of consciousness rather than the level of consciousness that connects us to the world, we begin to experience the beauty of Jesus' words, which make little sense from the perspective that the world has given us.

> Then someone came to him and said, "Teacher, what good deed must I do to have eternal life?" And he said to him, "Why do you ask me what is good? There is only one who is good. If you wish to enter into life, keep the commandments." He said to him, "Which ones?" And Jesus said, "You shall not murder; You shall not commit adultery; You shall not steal; You shall not bear false witness; Honor your father and your mother; also, You shall love your neighbor as yourself." The young man said to him, "I have kept all these; what do I still lack?" Jesus said to him, "If you wish to be perfect, go sell your possessions and give the money to the poor, and you will have treasure in heaven; then come, follow me." When the young man heard this word, he went away grieving, for he had many possessions.
>
> Then Jesus said to his disciples, "Truly I tell you, it is hard

for a rich person to enter the kingdom of heaven. Again I tell you it is easier for a camel to go through the eye of a needle than for someone who is rich to enter the kingdom of God." When the disciples heard this, they were greatly astounded and said, "Then who can be saved?" But Jesus looked at them and said, "For mortals it is impossible, but for God all things are possible."[15]

Jesus responds to the man's question, "What good deed must I do to have eternal life?"[16] by asking the man, "Why do you ask me about what is good? There is only one who is good."[17] God alone is good. Human beings seek what is good because the ego desires to be better than its neighbors and enemies. Jesus tells the man, "If you wish to enter into life, keep the commandments."[18] The man, however, insists on knowing specifically which commandments. So Jesus gives him a list of commandments. Jesus ends the list, however, by saying, "You shall love your neighbor as yourself."[19] The young man responds by claiming to have kept all these commandments, which Jesus knows is not true. Perhaps the man has not murdered anyone, committed adultery, or stolen anything, but have any of us loved our neighbor in the same way we love ourselves?

Instead of calling the man a liar for having claimed to love his neighbor in the same way we love himself, Jesus tells him, "If you wish to be perfect, go sell your possessions, and give the money to the poor, and you will have treasure in heaven; then come, follow me."[20]

The ego can claim righteousness by obeying most of the commandments, but loving our neighbor as ourselves is not something the ego can do. Neither does the ego find it easy to give away all its possessions since, its possessions are what make the ego better than its neighbors and its enemies. Being reduced to who we are in God and who God is in us only ultimately happens through the death of the ego, since if God tries to share space with a human being whose ego is still active, God's presence will inflate the ego and pervert what God is trying to do. What God is ultimately trying to accomplish is to bring his kingdom to earth through Jesus and his followers. Jesus was great at being God's empty vessel through whom God could pour his mercy, forgiveness, and love to the world. Jesus' followers, however, are in a vast variety of places in the spiritual journey where the ego is still very much alive.

What represents the real separation between Christians is not the doctrines they believe, but the places they are at on the spiritual journey and how stuck they are in those places. People closer to the end of the spiritual journey tend to be more sympathetic toward people in the earlier stages, since they can recall themselves getting stuck in such places and believing that righteousness was the end of the journey. Jesus, however, tells us that giving up everything and becoming those egoless instruments of God's mercy, forgiveness, and love to the world is the end of the journey, as it was for Jesus. This is the deeper life to which Jesus ultimately calls us. To that extent, God is calling us to the same life he called Jesus, the only difference being that Jesus accomplished the task perfectly, while we accomplish the task through repentance over Jesus' words, which results in our being overwhelmed with God's mercy, forgiveness, and love. All of this is intended to destroy the control the ego has upon our lives so we might realize God's greater purposes for our lives.

The way the above story ends is with Jesus' disciples asking Jesus, "Then who can be saved?"[21] If what is ultimately required is that we give up our possessions and be reduced to poverty then who can be saved? Of course, the ultimate point of the gospel is not to make us righteous, but to make us merciful and forgiving after having received much mercy and forgiveness at whatever point in the spiritual journey we might find ourselves. All that is required is that we pay attention to Jesus' words and repent over those words and thus be filled with his mercy and forgiveness, which overflows through us to the world.

---

1. Luke 14:26.
2. Luke 14:33.
3. John 3:7.
4. Matthew 18:1–4.
5. Luke 9:57–62.
6. John 14:20; John 15:4–5.
7. Matthew 22:37.
8. John 14:26.
9. 1st Timothy 1:15–16.
10. John 14:15–17.
11. John 15:1–5
12. Matthew 6:14–15.
13. Matthew 7:1–2.
14. John 14:26.
15. Matthew 19:16–26.
16. Matthew 19:16.
17. Matthew 19:17.
18. Matthew 19:17.
19. Matthew 19:19.
20. Matthew 19:21.
21. Matthew 19:25.

CHAPTER 8

SYNOPSIS OF THE SPIRITUAL JOURNEY AND THE DEEPER LIFE

The spiritual journey almost always begins with a belief that we believe makes us better in God's mind and our own mind than other people. It is natural that the spiritual journey begins with such a belief since we begin the spiritual journey from the perspective of the life we have created to be in the world, which is the life of the ego that has developed throughout our acculturation in the world. Why wouldn't the ego accept a belief that makes us better than other people? Becoming more than other people is what the ego and the world are all about.

Our earliest ideas of God are little more than who we imagine we would be if we were the creator and maintainer of the universe. From that perspective of who we would be if we were God, we would expect our creation to honor and worship us as God. If we are made in the image and likeness of God, God must have an ego, just like us, and being the greatest of all egos, God must demand honor and worship just as we would if we were God. This is the place and level of consciousness from which the Bible begins.

Jesus, however, tells a completely different story. Although claiming to be the son of God, Jesus rejects all the acclaim that we might imagine God, or the son of God, would want from his creation. Recall that when Jesus had fasted for forty days and nights, he was tempted to reveal that he was the Son of God by turning stones into loaves of bread. To which Jesus replied, "One does not live by bread alone."[1] The three temptations that the Devil set before Jesus were intended to prove that he was God's Son by showing himself to be more than other men. But Jesus was not more than other men—he was less than other men. Jesus lived at least throughout his public ministry without an ego and gave himself away to his Father's creation in the same way that his Father constantly gives himself away to his creation. This is also the life to which Jesus calls his followers. Giving ourselves away to God's creation and functioning without an ego is the deeper life to which Jesus calls his followers, but it takes a lifetime of dying to self-interest before we can truly love our neighbor and even our enemy in the same way we love ourselves. How close we come to this ultimate end to which Jesus calls us is what determines where we begin eternal life.

In the early stages of the spiritual journey, we are still operating out of the ego and its desire to be more than other people. Wanting to add righteousness to our beliefs is quite natural in the early stages of the spiritual journey, where we are still operating largely out of ego, which seeks to be more than other human beings rather than less. Jesus, however, resisted the temptations the devil set before him in the wilderness.[2] He refused to reveal himself to be more than other men in terms of power, esteem, and wealth, because by the time Jesus had begun his public ministry, he had completed the spiritual journey and had died to the temptations of the ego to be more than other men. Jesus, like his Father, has no ego, or at least by the time Jesus began his public ministry he had completed the spiritual journey and experienced the death of the ego and was able to give himself away to his Father's creation in the same way that his Father does.

God, the creator and maintainer of a universe, does not have an ego, but constantly gives himself away to his creation. God is love and we can participate in God's divine love by giving ourselves aways to others the way God gives himself away to his creation. God does not desire our worship, but desires that we would give ourselves away to his creation in acts of love, just as God does, and as Jesus' life depicts. This was The Way of the original first century church and it is the omega of human history toward which we are being divinely drawn.

God has made us in his own likeness with the ability to create our own eternal nature by the things we choose to love. Jesus tells us that God does not judge us. "The Father judges no one but has given all judgment to the Son."[3] Later in John's Gospel, Jesus tells us that he does not judge us, but that we do have a judge.

In the early stages of the spiritual journey, the ego is attracted to the idea that God judges us according to our beliefs and righteous behavior, which make us better than other human beings, but Jesus speaks of a deeper life where the living words of Jesus come to life within us. Unfortunately, the beauty of Jesus' words cannot even be seen from the perspective that our life in the world has given us. From the perspective that the world has given us it makes no sense to love our enemies[4] and give to all who beg from us.[5] But there is a deeper life from whose perspective we can see the beauty of Jesus' words and want those living words to take root within us and form the nature and character of our eternal being.

Jesus' words, however, also speak of the worst things to love, which interestingly are the very things that the world tells us are the best things to love. The words of Jesus, which tell us the best things to love, do not appeal to the person we have created to be in the world, and conversely, what Jesus tells us are the worst things to love are the very things that the world tells us are the things that we should love. Of course, we can avoid this dilemma by remaining in the early stages of the spiritual journey where we believe that our beliefs and righteous behavior are sufficient for a heavenly eternal life, but Jesus tells us that his words are what judge us[6] and determine how heavenly our eternal life will be. This is the enormous freedom that God has given to the human species: to create their own eternal being by the things we choose to love. Choosing to love those things that make us appear to be better than other people is what puts us in an eternal state of hell along with other beings who are eternally trying to be better than those beings with whom they share eternal life. However, giving ourselves away to others is what puts us with other eternal beings who give themselves to others through mercy, forgiveness, and love, just like Jesus.

As we have said, eternal life is not based upon the religious beliefs and righteous behavior that we believe make us better than other human beings, but upon how far we go into the deeper life to which Jesus calls us. Eternal life is a matter of God giving us our hearts' desire, so be careful about what your heart desires. Do we really want to spend eternity with beings who wish to have more wealth, power, prestige, beauty, strength, or righteousness than others? Or do we want to spend eternity with beings who are constantly giving themselves away in acts of mercy, forgiveness, and love?

God gives us whatever our hearts desire. Eternal life is a matter of sharing eternity with beings who love the things we love. This is what makes the words of Jesus so important and puts them on a different level than the rest of the Bible. Jesus' words tell us the best things to love and the worst things to love, since our hearts' desires, not our beliefs and behavior, are what shape our eternal being.

Our transformation into Jesus' followers is a matter of

getting beyond the beliefs and righteous behavior that we believe make us better than other people. It is a matter of practicing repentance over Jesus' words, which is always followed by the experience of God's mercy, forgiveness, and love. Repentance over Jesus' words is what keeps us on the journey, but we would see no need for repentance if not for the words of Jesus, which constantly reveal our sin at ever deeper levels. Of course, we can always choose to avoid the hard words of Jesus and simply trust our beliefs and righteousness to evade the necessity for repentance and the subsequent experience of God's mercy, forgiveness, and love always being deeper than our sin.

Our beliefs and behavior are under our control, but becoming God's mercy, forgiveness, and love to the world is something only God can do within us. Our only part in our transformation into Jesus' merciful, forgiving, and loving likeness is repentance over Jesus' words, which is always followed by God pouring forth his mercy, forgiveness, and love to the world through us. How much transformation we are up for is largely influenced by how much ego death we are willing to bear. The ego always strives to be more than other human beings, but Jesus is always calling his followers to be less than other human beings, devoid of ego so we might become those empty vessels through whom God's love, mercy, and forgiveness might freely flow to the world without interference from the self-interest of the ego. As we have said, Jesus was not more than other men, but less. He operated without the self-interest that usually directs our lives in the world. This is the deeper life to which Jesus is always calling us, but the ego usually does not die in one glorious instant. It takes a lifetime of surrender to God's greater purposes for our lives, turning away from those purposes that we concoct to make ourselves appear to be more than other human beings. This is the death of the ego that the great Christian saints and mystics have pursued for the last two thousand years. How far we go into this deeper life to which

Jesus calls us is determined by how much ego death we are willing to bear, and consequently how open we are to being the instruments of God's mercy, forgiveness, and love to the world.

If the ego is the dominant level of consciousness out of which we live our lives, we will cling to our beliefs and righteous behavior which the ego believes makes us better than other people. The ego can love much of the Bible, which in many places speaks of the early stages of the spiritual journey, but the ego cannot provide a place for Jesus' words to take root and produce heavenly fruit. For Jesus' words to take root within us, we must practice our deeper life of being in God and God being in us, until that deeper life becomes the dominant level of consciousness out of which we live our lives.

Of course, in opposition to this deeper life of being in God and God being in us, which Jesus promises his followers at the end of John's Gospel,[7] is the ego which we and the world have created to be in the world and to be in the world in a better state than our neighbors and our enemies. The message of the gospel, however, is to be less than our neighbors and our enemies. It is to become empty, angelic vessels through whom God pours his mercy, forgiveness, and love into the world. This is the ultimate end to which Jesus calls his followers. How far we proceed toward that end is what determines where we begin eternal life.

Prayer, at its deepest level, is a matter of identifying with that deeper life of being in God and God being in us. In the early stages of the spiritual journey, where we are still living out of the ego that we have created to be in the world, we believe the gospel and our belief in it makes us better than our neighbors and our enemies. But that is merely the ego's interpretation of the gospel, not the deeper life to which Jesus is calling us. The deeper life is devoid of ego, since ego is what prevents us from becoming an empty vessel through whom God's mercy, forgiveness, and love may pass to the world without interference from the judgments of the ego. This is the deeper life to which Jesus calls us, but it ultimately requires the death of the false self that we have created to be in the world, the false self that is always fixating on adding wealth, power, prestige, or religious beliefs and practices that make us appear superior to others. But Jesus gives us the perfect example of someone reduced to an empty vessel through whom God might reveal the nature of the Divine to the world. This is the ultimate end of the spiritual journey to which Jesus calls his followers. It is not about becoming more than others because of our beliefs and righteous behavior, but about being reduced to that angelic state of who we were before the world began insisting that we create a false self that is better than our neighbor and our enemy. How far we go into the depths of this deeper life is what determines the nature and character of where we begin eternal life. God allows us to judge ourselves by the things we choose to love. Loving the things that Jesus tells us to love creates an eternal being that resembles the Divine, while loving the things that the world tells us to love creates a hellish form of being.

We have been given enormous freedom to create the nature and character of our own eternal being by the things we choose to love. Jesus tells us the best things to love and the worst things to love. What is so strange about the words of Jesus is that what he tells us are the worst things to love are the very things the world tells us are the best things to love, because they make us appear to be more than our neighbors and our enemies.

The world tells us that it is good to have more wealth, power, prestige, and correct religious beliefs than others. But Jesus tells his followers that there is a deeper life of being in God and God being in us, rather than our being in the world and the world being in us. Being in God rather than being in the world does not add more to our life but reduces us to those empty vessels through whom God's love, mercy, and forgiveness might pass to the world unaffected by our judgments concerning who are worthy of love, mercy, and forgiveness. This is the deeper life to which Jesus calls his followers, but it ultimately requires the death of the false self that the ego creates to be in the world, and what's more, to be better than the rest of God's creation.

How far we go on the spiritual journey into this deeper life to which Jesus calls us is determined by how much we disidentify with the ego and the false self it creates to be in the world and instead identify with our deeper life in God and God in us. This is the deeper life that can give root to Jesus' words, but it must be practiced enough that we identify with it rather than the life we have created to be in the world. If we try to live the gospel out of the false self, anything we imagine God doing in our lives will tend to inflate the ego and cause us to see ourselves as more than other people rather than less.

The problem with believing that our beliefs and righteous behavior make us better than those who lack those beliefs and righteous behavior is that such beliefs and behavior inflate the ego and make it impossible to love our neighbor and our enemy in the same way we love ourselves. Getting beyond our beliefs and righteous behavior is what the deeper life is all about, but it ultimately requires the death of the ego so that our deeper life in God and God in us might come forth.

Prayer, at its deepest level, is the practice of this deeper life. If Jesus' living words are to take root within us, they cannot take root within the person we have created to be in the world, but only in that deeper life of who we were in God and who God was in us before the world demanded that we create an ego to make us more than our neighbors and our enemies. Getting back to that deeper life of who we were in God and who God was in us before the world began making us into its likeness is what the spiritual journey is all about.

The way we proceed into this deeper life to which Jesus calls us is not through a path of righteousness whereby we practice the avoidance of sin, but by seeing our sin on ever deeper levels so we might experience God's mercy and forgiveness on ever deeper levels. Jesus says,

> Do not think that I have come to abolish the law and the prophets; I have come not to abolish but to fulfill. For truly I tell you, until heaven and earth pass away, not one letter, not one stroke of a letter, will pass from the law until all is accomplished.[8]

Strangely, what follows this statement throughout the rest of the Sermon on the Mount, and the rest of the gospel in general, is Jesus giving numerous examples of his words seeming to contradict and destroy what had been set forth by the law and the prophets who proceeded him. He constantly refers to the law and the prophets by saying what the law and the prophets said, following that with, "But I say to you...."[9] Jesus follows the phrase, "But I say to you" with something quite different from what the law and the prophets said. Jesus says, "I have come not to abolish but to fulfill,"[10] but then follows that by making statements that seem to contradict the law and the prophets. So what is going on?

Jesus is always talking about truth as a way of being rather than truth as something to know and believe. Of course, our modern culture has taught us to think of truth as something to know rather than something to be. Our modern culture has taught us that the best way to know is the way we know mathematics—as objective, certain, and precise. Many of the modern forms of Christianity have endorsed this notion of truth as something objective, certain, and precise, rather than The Way that Jesus taught his followers to be.

Truth, as a way of being, is never objective, certain, or precise. Rather, it is a matter of discovering life on ever deeper levels from which we can see the beauty of Jesus' words and increasingly want those living words to come to life within us. Our ability to move to those deeper levels of being in God rather than being in the world ultimately requires the death of the life that we have created for ourselves to be in the world. This dying of the ego life that we have created to be in the world is what allows us to get beyond our beliefs and attempts at righteousness and gives us a taste of the deeper life of being in God and God being in us.

Unfortunately, our initial experiences of this deeper life of being in God and God being in us will tend to inflate whatever ego has not died and cause us to see ourselves as more than other people rather than less. Of course, we are fine with that so long as we avoid the words of Jesus, since so much of the Bible is speaking to the early stages of the spiritual journey and not the deeper life to which Jesus' words are always calling us. This deeper life to which Jesus calls his followers does initially have the negative effect of inflating the ego as is revealed in the lives of Jesus' own disciples, who vied for places of importance amongst themselves.

> A dispute arose among them as to which one of them was to be regarded as the greatest. But he said to them, "The kings of the gentiles lord it over them, and those in authority over them are called benefactors. But not so with you; rather the greatest among you must become like the youngest, and the leader like one who serves. For who is greater, the one who is at the table or the one who serves? Is it not the one at the table? But I am among you as one who serves.[11]

In a similar place Jesus is asked,

> Who is the greatest in the kingdom of heaven? He called a child, whom he put amongst them, and said, "Truly I tell you, unless you change and become like children, you will never

enter the kingdom of heaven. Whoever becomes humble like this child is greatest in the kingdom of heaven."[12]

Getting back to who we were in God and who God was in us before the world began insisting that we show ourselves to be more than our neighbors and our enemies is what the spiritual journey and the deeper life are all about. The way back to this deeper life is through the death of the ego that we and the world have created to be better than our neighbors and our enemies, rather than their servants, like Jesus.

The purpose of the ego is to establish itself as better than others. Our religious beliefs and righteous behavior appeal to the ego, and we can find support for the ego throughout most of the Bible, but the ego will always be repulsed by the hard words of Jesus, since Jesus is not telling us how to be righteous in the world, but rather, how to bring his kingdom to earth. This is the purpose of the gospel, and that purpose ultimately requires the death of the ego. We would like to believe that the ego died when we accepted Jesus into our lives, but the death of the ego is a slow and arduous process, which usually doesn't even begin for years and even decades after it has been created through our acculturation as children, adolescents, and young adults. Dying to the person we have created to be in the world is the only way back to who we were in God and who God was in us before the world started making us into its likeness by being better than our neighbors and our enemies. Being better than other human beings is not the deeper life to which Jesus calls his followers, but it takes years of repenting over Jesus' words before we even begin to see the deeper life. Only the words of Jesus, and our repentance over them, gets us beyond the early stages of the spiritual journey where we can get stuck in our beliefs and righteousness. The deeper life to which Jesus calls us is impossible from the life and level of consciousness that we have created for ourselves to be in the world. The deeper life is meant to get us beyond the superficial life that the world tells us is so important because it is what makes us different from one another. But Jesus is always calling us to see how very much the same we all are. This is the deeper life to which Jesus calls us, and getting back to it is what prayer is all about at its deepest contemplative level. The silence and stillness of prayer is what get us back to that deepest level of consciousness that we share with every other human being before the world insisted that we be different and better than others. This is the deeper life that we practice in contemplative prayer, but the sin of the world keeps us from living out of that deeper level of consciousness that we all shared with every other human being before the world began making us into its likeness.

> When a lawyer asked Jesus, "Which commandment in the law is the greatest?" Jesus said,
> "You shall love the Lord your God with all your heart, and with all your soul, and with all your mind." This is the greatest and first commandment. And a second is like it: "You shall love your neighbor as yourself." On these two commandments hang all the law and the prophets.

When considered closely, both commandments make righteousness impossible. If all the love in our heart, soul, and mind is to be directed toward God and nothing else, as it was with Jesus, there is no love left over for ourselves or anything else. Jesus' point is that "there is no one who is righteous, not even one."[13] Likewise, there is no one who loves their neighbor in the same way that they love themselves. The point that both Jesus and Paul are making is that, although righteousness may be a goal which we pursue in the early stages of the journey, it is unrealistic and serves only to inflate the ego. The deeper life is always about seeing our sin at ever deeper levels so we can experience God's mercy, forgiveness, and love at ever deeper levels. The end to which Jesus calls us is to progressively become more and more merciful, forgiving, and loving for having experienced so much mercy, forgiveness, and love ourselves by seeing our sin at ever deeper levels.

God does not judge us but allows us to judge ourselves by the way we judge others. "Do not judge, so that you may not be judged. For with the judgment you make you will be judged, and the measure you give will be the measure you get."[14] God forgives everyone because God is forgiving and merciful, but our eternal state is determined by how forgiving and merciful we become, and that is determined by how much forgiveness and mercy we have received because of our paying attention to Jesus' words and the repentance to which his words call us.

God forgives everyone's sin because God is forgiving, but how forgiving and merciful we become is dependent upon how much forgiveness and mercy we are aware of receiving. This is the deeper life of the spiritual journey, where forgiveness and mercy take us beyond righteousness. The path to this deeper life is through the hard words of Jesus which reveal our sin at ever deeper levels, but also reveal that God's mercy and forgiveness are always deeper still.

Righteousness, like belief, is acquired in an early place in the journey, but we only get to the deep places in the journey by paying attention to the hard words of Jesus, which reveal our sin on ever deeper levels so we might experience God's mercy and forgiveness on those deeper levels. Jesus points out the sin of righteousness in several different places in Luke's Gospel. In the parable of the Pharisee and the tax collector,[15] Jesus compares a righteous man with a repentant sinner who experiences God's mercy and forgiveness in a way that the righteous man does not. The experience of mercy and forgiveness are only open to sinners who pay attention to Jesus' words, which reveal our sin at ever deeper levels. This alone is what opens us to the ever-deeper experiences of God's transformative mercy and forgiveness.

The same point is made with the story of the Prodigal Son,[16] where the righteous older brother never experiences the mercy and forgiveness that his sinful brother does. Of course, the point is not that we should sin, but that if we pay attention to Jesus' words, we see that there is no end to our sin, and likewise no end to God's mercy and forgiveness if we seek them by paying attention to Jesus' words.

Likewise in the Parable of the Good Samaritan,[17] where Jesus shows that, while righteousness is thought of merely as the avoidance of sin, mercy is godlike. Today, our opposition to abortion and homosexuality are good indicators that we are stuck in righteousness. Mercy and forgiveness always trump righteousness and represent deeper places in the spiritual journey.

---

1. Matthew 4:4.
2. Matthew 4:1–11.
3. John 5:22
4. Matthew 5:44.
5. Matthew 5:42.
6. John 12:47–48.
7. John 14–17.
8. Matthew 5:17–18.
9. Matthew 5:22, 5:28, 5:32, 5:34, 5:39. 5:44.
10. Matthew 5:17.
11. Luke 22:24–27.
12. Matthew 18:1–4.
13. Romans 3:10.
14. Matthew 7:1–2.
15. Luke 18:10–14.
16. Luke 15:11–32.
17. Luke 10:25–42.

EPILOGUE

Saints are not people who go to heaven when they die because they believed the right things and are righteous, but people who bring Jesus' kingdom to earth because they experience the progressive death of the ego, which allows them to give themselves to the interests of others, just like Jesus, through acts of mercy, forgiveness, and love. This is the fullness of life to which Jesus calls his followers, but the only way to come into this fullness of life in God is through spiritual poverty—that is, giving ourselves away to others, be it your wife, your children, or the stranger on the street. This is the deeper life and level of consciousness that alone can see the beauty of Jesus' words to forgive everyone,[1] judge no one,[2] and love even your enemies.[3]

The key to this deeper life is about practicing the poverty of spirit,[4] which ultimately brings about the ever-increasing death to the ego, in order that our deeper life in God and God in us might come forth. Practicing this deeper life is what contemplative prayer or the practice of silence is all about. This practice takes years to develop, since early in the practice, our experience of God's presence in prayer tends to inflate the ego, rather than to reduce us to those empty vessels through whom God's mercy, forgiveness, and love might freely flow to the world.

This is why Jesus tells us that we will be blessed if we "hunger and thirst for righteousness"[5] rather than believing that righteousness is something that we already have through our beliefs and behavior. Jesus' words are always calling us to a deeper life that ultimately involves the death of the ego, because the living words of Jesus can never take root in the person we have created to be in the world. The end of the spiritual journey to which Jesus calls us is the deeper life that is able to give root to Jesus' words, but it usually takes a lifetime for that to happen because the deeper life only comes forth with the death of the false self that we have created to be in the world, and to be better in the world than our neighbors and our enemies.

The reason a deeper life is required is because from the perspective the world has given us it is impossible to see the beauty of Jesus words. Jesus' words are repulsive to the person we have created to be in the world. To give to all who ask[6] or to love even our enemies[7] makes no sense from the level of consciousness that connects us to the world, but there is a deeper level of consciousness that connects us to who we were in God and who God was in us before the world began making us into its likeness, but this deeper life must be practiced if it is to become the dominant level of consciousness with which we identify. The way we practice this deeper life is through the prayer of silence. Silence is what disconnects us from that level of consciousness that connects us to the world, instead providing a perspective that allows us to see the beauty of Jesus' words. From the perspective the world has given us it makes no sense to forgive everyone, judge no one, and love even your enemies, but from the perspective of who we are in God and who God is in us, these are the most beautiful words ever spoken.

The way this transformation into a deeper level of consciousness and a deeper level of being occurs is by paying attention to the words of Jesus, which not only reveal our sin at ever deeper levels, but also reveal that God's forgiveness and mercy are always deeper still. What prevents this transformation from happening are popular religious beliefs that tell us our only problem is that we have sinned and need to get our sins forgiven through our belief that Jesus on the cross has paid for our sins. It is the belief that our sins are the only thing keeping us from the fullness of life in God.

What makes this Salvation Gospel so attractive is that it means we can have the fullness of life promised by both God and the world. There are plenty of Old Testament scriptures to support that view. Jesus, however, is offering a very different message. He is not telling us how to be righteous in this world, but how to bring his kingdom to earth. Of course, from the perspective the world has given us, we are not interested in bringing Jesus' kingdom to earth. We just want to know what we must believe to go to heaven when we die. That is as much as we wish to know from the perspective of who we are in the world. But there is the deeper perspective of who we are in God and who God is in us. Practicing that deeper life is what prayer at its deepest level is all about.

Jesus, and not the Bible, is the word of God.[8] Of course, there is a way to understand that the Bible is the word of God, since life is a spiritual journey, and since the Bible speaks to the multiple places in that journey. It is all the word of God, so long as we stay on the journey and keep moving toward its end: the living words of Jesus, which are meant to take root at the deepest core of our being and produce the fruit that brings his kingdom to earth. This is what the great Christian saints and mystics have always understood. The greatest sin is wealth, or whatever makes you greater than other people, and our greatest virtue is poverty, or whatever reduces us to what we have in common with every other child of God that has come into the world. Giving ourselves away to the world in acts of mercy, forgiveness, and love, just like Jesus, is the blessed life. But it requires a lifetime of allowing the false self to die, the false self that we have created to make ourselves feel greater than God's other children.

---

1. Matthew 6:14–15.
2. Matthew 7:1–2.
3. Matthew 5:44.
4. Matthew 5:3.
5. Matthew 5:6.
6. Matthew 5:42.
7. Matthew 5:44.
8. John 1:1–4.

www.ingramcontent.com/pod-product-compliance
Lightning Source LLC
Chambersburg PA
CBHW031334160426
43196CB00007B/688